Creative Repair

Creative Repair

Pastoral Care and Creativity

Anne C. Holmes

scm press

© Anne C. Holmes 2023
Published in 2023 by SCM Press
Editorial office
3rd Floor, Invicta House,
108–114 Golden Lane,
London EC1Y 0TG, UK
www.scmpress.co.uk

SCM Press is an imprint of Hymns Ancient & Modern Ltd
(a registered charity)

Hymns Ancient & Modern® is a registered trademark of
Hymns Ancient & Modern Ltd
13A Hellesdon Park Road, Norwich,
Norfolk NR6 5DR, UK

British Library Cataloguing in Publication data
A catalogue record for this book is available
from the British Library

ISBN 978-0-334-06176-2

Typeset by Regent Typesetting
Printed and bound in Great Britain by
CPI Group (UK) Ltd

Contents

For Simon and Rachel

Foreword

The theme of this book is beautifully summed up in its title, *Creative Repair*. So many of us, perhaps all of us, are in need of repair, either because of some trauma we are going through now or that we experienced earlier in life; or even perhaps because we are suffering the long-term effects of trauma in the lives of our parents and forebears. Its hopeful theme is that repair is available not just through therapy, but also by engaging in some form of creative activity. Examples from music are given, such as playing an instrument or, especially, choral music; and also drawing and theatre. These activities allow a person to relax and simply do what they enjoy doing, thereby releasing fresh springs of creativity within them. The theme is vividly illustrated in the Japanese art of *kintsugi*, whereby a broken dish is not thrown away but repaired with gold and becomes more valued than the original.

This is the best kind of book: drawn from her own experience of pain and difficulty, about which the author is honest; the fruit of extensive training and practice as a clinician, and its associated literature; drawing on some vivid personal histories; and imbued with a sure practical wisdom. All these qualities are directed to enabling clergy, especially those suffering stress or experiencing burnout, to recover the freshness and enthusiasm of ministry.

The practical wisdom of this book, what the Greeks prized as *phronesis*, is suggested by three of its key concepts: well-being, balance and time wisdom, words which seem particularly relevant to busy clergy. It is a book that will be helpful both to those engaged in helping others through therapy and to those in ministry.

Richard Harries

Acknowledgements

I would like to thank all those who supported me during the original research and who have since encouraged me to write this book.

All the participants in my doctoral research.

My colleagues Val Parker and Jill Buckledee who have been central to my writing the initial proposal and for offering critical encouragement as I completed the manuscript.

The Rt Revd Lord Harries of Pentregarth for writing the Foreword.

My former doctoral supervisors, the Revd Dr Jane Leach and Dr Zoë Bennett who provided insight, wisdom, encouragement and support.

My friend Trisha Dale for reading some of the chapters and especially for completing the index.

My clinical supervisors Mrs Sheila Mackintosh Millard and the Revd Professor Alistair Ross.

Sister Paula, Abbess, and the Sisters of the Community of St Clare, Freeland, Oxfordshire.

Dear friends who have variously encouraged, fed and prayed with and for me throughout this process, especially Pat, Marilyn, Cathy, Becky, Laura, Nicola, Paula, Tricia and Siân.

My son, Simon, and daughter-in-law, Kate; my daughter, Rachel, and son-in-law, Mark, and their families. Also, my sister, Jennifer, and brother-in-law, John, and their family.

David Shervington and his team at SCM Press, especially Rachel Geddes.

I

Introduction

This book is the result of many years of thinking and research. As a psychotherapist and Anglican priest, I have worked with people from a wide variety of backgrounds who may or may not have professed a religious faith. My interest in the importance of creativity first found expression in a theoretical paper written when training as a group psychotherapist in the early 1990s. I had observed that there was a link between blocked grief and blocked creativity, and noticed that when a person was able to unblock their grief they also released their creative energy. This applied both to individuals in counselling and people being helped in group therapy. For example, I once worked with a writer whose capacity to write was blocked by unprocessed grief since a parent had died. When these feelings of loss had been sufficiently released, I was thanked for my help and the work was brought to an end because the writing had resumed. Another example was a graduate student who kept deleting his work as he tried to write up his thesis. He was in a group with others who had different problems and they helped him to understand the underlying family grief issues that were blocking his progress and, in time, he found a way of saving his work for future editing, rather than deleting it all as soon as he had written it. He went on to complete his thesis and be awarded his doctorate.

In the past, my roles as a clinician and a Christian leader were kept separate. In order to be fully available for our clients, it is usual for counsellors and psychotherapists to keep personal information away from the therapy sessions. While that is still the case from a clinical point of view, I later combined the two disciplines academically in an MA in Pastoral Theology. Seeking a topic for the dissertation, I began by exploring the connection between involvement in the creative arts and a pastor's or carer's capacity to restore energy expended in sensitive pastoral care. The idea of *creative repair* began to form in my mind at a time in my life when I was dealing with the complicated grief following the death of my former husband nearly 20 years after we had separated. The concept emerged from a personal reflection during the grieving process and began in France on 19 August 2007. It was the day on which the ashes of my former husband were to be scattered off Spithead, as he had requested before his death. As he had remarried it was not appropriate for me to be there. I was in my holiday cottage in north Burgundy, intentionally reflecting on our marriage and honouring the happier times. One of our common interests had been a love of music, especially choral church music and organ music. I was listening to a recording of organ music and recognizing that this music stretched back to the beginning of my life.

My father was an Anglican priest and church musician, having played the organ for services since the age of 13. Among my earliest memories are those of him playing the piano as I went to sleep. The music included Bach preludes and fugues, Beethoven sonatas and various pieces by Brahms and Chopin. As I thought about him, I realized that his music was for him both a release and a resource because he never talked about the various pastoral encounters of his ministry. Had my father intuitively known that music was the safe container for both personal difficulties and the emotional demands of being a priest? I knew that his childhood was difficult, that he would rarely speak of his experience as an RAF chaplain in the Far East during the Second World War, and that he had had the unpleasant task of exposing and bringing to justice the perpetrators of a paedophile ring in one of his parishes. He had played the organ in church and the piano in jazz bands as a young man, and played both instruments throughout his life. He worked hard but never experienced burnout. Gradually, as

I grieved and reflected, the idea of the role of the creative arts in the restoration of energy expended in pastoral care became clear. I set out to explore the idea and my future studies represented further exploration of the role of creativity in the sustaining of ministry.

In order to explore this idea further in a research context, I conducted a focus group of volunteer clergy. I devised a series of questions and recorded their spontaneous answers in a recorded discussion. Others who were interested but were unable to attend the focus group were sent a questionnaire by email (see Appendix A) and invited to respond. I was curious about the role that the creative arts might have played in their avoidance of extreme stress. For some, such stress can accumulate until a person suffers from burnout, a type of breakdown from which it can take months, if not years, to recover. Two of those who responded had already experienced burnout and had found that participation in creativity, whether reading novels or learning a new craft, had been crucial in their recovery and had since then become part of their regular way of life.

The recognition by colleagues of the value of this early research led to further doctoral studies. Another focus group confirmed the value of creative repair and also indicated the role of other people sharing a dance group or an online game, which highlighted the additional value of being in a creative repair group for some people. Later in-depth interviews with a few clergy in a leadership role indicated the importance of belonging to a group outside a working or ministry context. The need to practise creative repair regularly was central to its ongoing value, so that it become part of spiritual practice. The theological significance of creativity came through as people spoke of the wish to follow the example of Jesus in taking a break from active ministry. Some saw it as participating in God's ongoing Creation, thus becoming intentional co-creators with God.

This book is a continuation of this work and a response to the commitment to make the concept of creative repair better known. I believe that creative repair is an essential practice for anyone involved with helping others. This includes those in a parenting role who often need permission to take time out for themselves and renew the interests which they may have pursued before they became parents. In addition to new writing, the material in this book has been drawn partly from my doctoral research and partly from the preceding MA dissertation and published papers. In addition, I have reflected on many workshops conducted among clergy, ordinands, counsellors and singing teachers, as well as countless conversations with family, friends and colleagues, both lay and ordained. Underlying my thinking has been the experience of working as a group analyst, psychodynamic counsellor, supervisor and spiritual director over the last 35 years.

The following summaries give an idea of the reader's path through the rest of the book.

In Chapter 2 I introduce the concept of creative repair – its origins and meaning. This draws on the creative arts and therapies and explains the meaning of 'repair' in psychoanalysis. The connection between grief and creativity is explored.

Chapter 3 is a consideration of the need for self-care for those working in a pastoral or therapeutic context. This includes some of the literature on well-being and resilience as applied to these contexts. Readers are invited to do an informal audit of what resources them and drains them.

Individual creative repair is considered in Chapter 4. This was where my studies began. It outlines the importance of this, drawing on qualitative research undergone for academic purposes and including composite case studies drawn from clinical work.

Chapter 5 highlights the importance of creative repair in a group. It considers the additional and substantial benefits of practising it with others. This will embrace both the particular needs of clergy based in their parish setting and ways in which counsellors and other therapists routinely resource themselves.

In Chapter 6 the creative repair of things considers a non-materialistic view of objects which carry meaning, memories and transgenerational continuity.

The practice of creative repair involves the development of rhythms to support it. This is the focus of Chapter 7, which affirms the importance of developing new habits of rhythm and discipline. In order to be effective, creative repair needs to be practised regularly. Reference is made to the monastic tradition and the increasing interest in having a rule of life.

Chapter 8 considers the popular idea of resilience and the contribution that creative repair makes to it. Some of the literature on resilience can be enhanced by the introduction of various ways of being creative.

Although implicit theology runs throughout the book, Chapter 9 is more explicit about a theology of creative repair. It draws on feedback from study days and weekend retreats on spirituality and creative repair.

Chapter 10, the concluding chapter, gathers up the themes of the book and advocates an intentional introduction of creative repair into mainstream ministry and pastoral practice. It stresses the importance of beginnings and the need to build good practice into formation and training, as well as regular review of practice and professional development. It also indicates the universal potential of creative repair to resource anyone involved in caring for others, whether in a formal role or informally as parents or other caregivers. As a concept and practice, creative repair is here to stay.

2

The Concept of Creative Repair

The concept of creative repair can be defined as regular, active engagement with the creative arts as a way of repairing energy expended in sensitive pastoral care. However much the pastoral carer enjoys the work, the act of listening attentively to someone's story, which often includes painful experiences, uses up emotional and psychological energy. How does the listener restore this energy? I believe that, in addition to the obvious need to rest, some form of participation in the creative arts, such as sitting down with a novel, watching a programme or doing some knitting, depending on the person's interests, can contribute to that restoration. The origin of the concept involves some difficult and specialist knowledge drawn from the history and practice of psychoanalysis. For example, creative repair combines on the one hand the psychoanalytic idea of *repair*, in a here-and-now encounter, of the damage done to the psyche in formative relationships and, on the other, the capacity of the *creative* arts to restore emotional and psychological energy. In this chapter I will draw attention to the importance of the creative arts and explain how the word 'repair' is usefully drawn from psychoanalysis as shorthand for the way in which we can be restored by our engagement with a wide range of creative activities. In addition, I will explore the relationship between grief and creativity.

There have been artists for as long as there have been human beings. The human capacity to symbolize is ancient, as cave paintings such as those of Lascaux have shown us (Gombrich, 1953). In his film *How Art Began* (shown on BBC Two on 26 January 2019), sculptor Anthony Gormley concludes:

If this film of ours can convey anything, it's the sense of this emergent truth that art was there right from the beginning ... that art is intrinsic to who we are, that art is probably our better part and that in some way, when uncaptured by political or economic interest, it expresses a joy in being, a connection with all living beings, an awareness of the is-ness, but the absolute and utter need to join it, to make it and in that making, to register our extraordinary ability to reflect on existence.

Ancient texts from many cultures indicate the importance of poetry, music and dance. As one scholar has put it:

The urge to make and enjoy art seems to be universal: the impulse to scratch out images on stone walls, revel in the delight of notes strung together, shape and re-shape words into patterns and so on. (Begbie, 2001, p. xi)

Narrative and storytelling have long been means of recalling past events, whether individual or collective. It can happen in families, when younger members of the family ask their elderly relatives to talk about the past. Historical researchers seek to tell stories on behalf of communities. Increasingly the therapeutic importance of narrative is recognized in theology because it 'is now frequently claimed that the work of story-telling lies at the heart of the healing encounter between those who suffer and those who seek to meet this suffering with the resources of faith' (Walton, 2014, p. 164).

In addition to the creative arts, the human capacity to symbolize is experienced in dreams and daydreams, as evidenced by Freud (1991) and successive psychoanalysts. Judeo-Christian biblical narratives have given significance to dreams, often as game-changers for the dreamers. A famous example in the Hebrew Scriptures is the story of Joseph with his capacity to interpret the dreams of Pharaoh. The popularity of the musical *Joseph and the Amazing Technicolour Dreamcoat*, with lyrics by Tim Rice and music by Andrew Lloyd Webber, testifies to the continuing power of this biblical narrative. Currently there is a general acceptance of the importance of dreams in therapeutic encounters. One psychoanalyst in particular, Hannah Segal, focused on the importance of symbol formation (Segal, 1986).

The value of the creative arts in repairing wounded psyches has been evidenced at a professional level by the development of branches of psychotherapy that have become established disciplines in their own right. These include art therapy, music therapy and drama therapy. Art therapy is often used to help those with serious mental health problems. In a key text, *Art as Therapy*, Edith Kramer and her colleagues, especially Lani Gerity, explore definitions, emphasize the quality of the work practised, and focus on the inner unity of the process and art product 'with its miraculously integrating effects on the creator' (Gerity, 2000a, p. 10). Gerity gives an example of a 48-year-old woman survivor of sexual abuse who was working with clay alongside others in a group. She is quoted as saying:

> The day I put my hands into the clay and started creating a head of a person who is very dear to me, something magical happened. I felt a connection to a deep part of myself. I could put everything into this clay – my love, my anger, my fears – and create a thing of beauty. My soul was validated in an object I could touch, feel, look at. I felt a deep sense of self-worth, and even self-love. And this, after all, is the goal of my rehabilitation – to learn to cherish and love myself – from this everything else flows.

The art therapist comments: 'These patients, normally the most difficult to work with, while using clay were also clearly working on integration, feelings of wholeness and well-being' (Gerity, 2000b, p. 235). This example demonstrates the way in which the relationship between an art therapist and their patient can facilitate the repair of a fractured relationship, in this case as a result of early sexual abuse. I have drawn on such therapeutic work involving the creative arts as a key source for my concept of creative repair.

The therapeutic potential of art can impact not only on individuals, but can also contribute to the healing of those caught up in cultural crises. Within art therapy, the social significance of art is implied in Kramer's credo as an artist and an art therapist (Kramer, 2000): 'I see my tasks as an artist of our time to be twofold and interwoven: to celebrate that which is perishable and endangered, and to nourish and cultivate the capacity for experiencing' (p.15). Troubled by the 'screams and whisperings of seductive promises, admonitions and threats of the advertising industry and of politics', she goes on to counsel us to disregard these stimuli (p.15). Art and psychotherapy both imply a search for inner truth. All art is to be seen as therapeutic in the broadest sense of the word. Kramer writes: 'Since human society has existed the arts have helped man to reconcile the external conflict between the individual's instinctive urges and the demands of society' (p. 17). Although she did not experience the Nazi concentration camps herself, Kramer was deeply affected by the murders of Jewish teachers and colleagues, notably Dicker-Brandeis who taught art to children in the camp of Terezin. Some of Dicker-Brandeis's lectures about the teaching of art to children survived along with their art, 'testifying to the sustaining and healing power of art' (p. 21).

During the recent pandemic the therapeutic value of being creative has been highlighted by the way in which many people turned to various aspects of creativity in order to cope with the need to stay at home during the various periods of lockdown. One popular response has been *Grayson Perry's Art Club*. During two periods of lockdown he and his wife Philippa, a psychotherapist, hosted a series of programmes, each with a particular theme, in which viewers were invited to submit their own works of art. In each programme he invited a celebrity to choose her or his favourite three items for inclusion in his exhibition. He also chose his own favourites and conducted a virtual interview with the people who had made them. What was almost palpable was the sense of pleasure and privilege in the reaction of those he contacted, especially when he told them that he wanted to include their work in the exhibition. Meanwhile both he and Philippa made their own artefact on whichever theme was the focus of each programme. The inclusive nature of their approach was intended to make art accessible to all.

Sometimes I work with people whose primary occupation is that of practising the arts professionally. The role of the therapy is then more about helping them to reconcile conflicting aspects of their internal world, which has the effect of helping them to be more integrated in the expression of their art. Occasionally someone has come to see me because their access to their creativity has become blocked. This may be as a result of an important life event. One writer had become blocked after giving birth. It was as if all her creativity had been expressed in the literal act of bringing a new human being into the world. It had also stirred unconscious difficulties in her own early relationship with her mother. After a few weeks of work, she was able to write again and found her ongoing creative repair in the act of writing, so no longer needed to see me.

Talking to the British Voice Association

Those who work as music teachers, especially those working with individuals, often find themselves offering informal pastoral care. I have experienced this at first hand with my own singing teachers over the years. As the instrument is the body itself, suppressed or blocked feelings can impact on the way in which the voice can be used. For the last few years, I have taken part in the research of my teacher and friend, Rebecca Moseley-Morgan, who is particularly interested in the ageing voice. I was curious about the way in which she and her colleagues practise creative repair. As a result, I was invited to give a talk to the British Voice Association (BVA) in London on 30 January 2016 on the danger of burnout. As preparation for the talk, I contacted a few colleagues for whom singing, usually in a choir, was an essential part of their life. I invited them to reflect on their experience and they gave me permission to quote them anonymously. Their comments, whether to do with their own personal needs or as a support to their work, included the following:

'I sing to recover from work! It is my way of being extrovert to balance the introversion of the work. So I couldn't do without it.'

'A different mode of learning, risk and experiment from day-to-day pastoral (or academic, or managerial) engagement – which informs every other engagement with a much deeper, more "attuned" self-awareness that is deeply rooted in the body.'

'I think singing definitely helps me to breathe consciously and allows my voice to function as well as it can when in sessions with clients, rather than falling into mirroring the client who is suffocating or struggling with breathing through anxiety.'

The reference to mirroring gives access to what might be happening in a singing lesson, or in any one-to-one encounter in a professional context. The psychoanalytic ideas of transference and countertransference are becoming better known outside therapeutic circles. They are particularly important in the context of pastoral care (see Chapter 3 for a fuller application of this to pastoral care). When people come to us, whether for a lesson, or some sort of help, they bring with them, at an unconscious level, all their previous experiences of needing care or seeking help, going right back to their entry into the world. It is important for the tutor or caregiver to know what might be going on besides the singing lesson or pastoral encounter. Receiving projections from others can be very tiring and ignorance of this may leave us drained or depleted emotionally and psychologically.

In psychotherapy, a key element of the work is to help someone to find their own voice. In group therapy this is complicated by the need to find one's own voice in the presence of others who wish to do the same. One of the things therapists can offer is the capacity to listen without the need to judge or fix what is wrong. The very fact of having got something off one's chest actually changes how we feel. Some people have never been listened to in this way. It may be a consequence of being the youngest child in a large family. Sometimes I see people who have a dominant twin, so that they have had to retreat into themselves and adapt to the needs of others in order to survive. The singing teachers at the BVA study day were aware in a technical way that the tone or pitch of one's voice can betray what we are feeling. I remember that when my daughter was a teenager and young adult, it was often the flatness in her voice which gave me a clue as to what might be going on. In my clinical work, one patient notices that when she is distressed her voice becomes more high-pitched, and when it is lower she is more anchored in herself.

Some of my colleagues indicated the importance of knowing about singing and breathing. For example, one wrote:

'My knowledge of singing and voice production allows me to observe the sound of the client's voice and their breathing in order to see what might be causing unspoken anxiety, such as a strangled sound, an abnormally loud sound, a tiny voice in a large person.'

Singing in a choir can be very reparative for a therapist. One colleague said that she experienced physical repair in the body through singing because it is so physical. Singing offers repair from the many projections encountered in therapeutic work, because it is so centred in the body rather than the mind. We routinely work with splitting and fragmentation, whereas singing, especially choral singing, is about bringing the voices together – it's very integrating and an antidote to fragmentation. It is also good to be in the other role as the one who may have a powerful transference to the conductor. The capacity to be in another role and be on the receiving end is a key aspect of creative repair. As another colleague put it:

'Working with a master-coach, learning to go on unlearning and learning, allowing myself to be known in failure and frustration as well as in freedom and flow.'

The idea of being in a different role is one of the by-products of the work of Gareth Malone. His formation of various choirs has helped to increase the popularity of singing. Notable is the choir of Military Wives, whose moving performances highlighted the difficulty of being at home while their husbands were on active service. Whatever the rank of their respective husbands, the wives sang as one group. Similarly, in hospitals and other organizations in which staff were part of hierarchies, all were differentiated only by being sopranos, altos, tenors or basses as Malone rehearsed them for their performances. Not only were individuals helped to become less tense and more confident, but the non-hierarchical nature of the choirs fostered better relationships and communication within the organizations (Malone, 2012).

As part of the BVA talk, after introducing the concept of creative repair and giving a brief explanation of the need for singing teachers and others to resource themselves in a regular way, I invited the participants to talk to those near them about their way of doing this. As they were professional musicians, they tended not to find more music helpful. Their feedback indicated the importance of hobbies such as cooking and gardening, walking and various forms of sport, as well as reading and painting. While not all of these fell into the category of the creative arts, it was clear that the participants valued these various activities. What emerged was the value of knowing that it was a matter of professional obligation and integrity to make regular time for them and not see them as a luxury that could not be justified.

Many people expressed their deep sense of loss during the pandemic, of the opportunity to sing in choirs, play in bands or orchestras or go to listen to live music. It had been a terrible time for those who earn their living within the creative arts, despite many imaginative and quite brilliantly innovative ways of performing remotely. At the first night of the 2021 season of the BBC Promenade Concerts, the presence of a live audience gave a sense of huge relief to performers, whether members of the socially distanced orchestra, choir or soloists. One of the works performed was the 'Serenade to Music' by Ralph Vaughan Williams, a setting of words by William Shakespeare:

How sweet the moonlight sleeps upon this bank!
Here will we sit, and let the sounds of music
Creep in our ears: soft stillness and the night
Become the touches of sweet harmony.
Look, how the floor of heaven
Is thick inlaid with patines of bright gold:
There's not the smallest orb that thou behold'st
But in his motion like an angel sings
Still quiring to the young-eyed cherubins;
Such harmony is in immortal souls ...
It is your music of the house.

The combination of the words by one master of his art and the music of another served to help both those among the live audience and those of us taking part remotely to celebrate the re-entry of live Promenade Concerts after a year of deprivation and minimal attendance. Not only heaven but nature herself are included in the final words:

Soft stillness and the night
Become the touches of sweet harmony.
(*Merchant of Venice*, act 5, scene 1)

Listening to music, whether live or recorded, is one of the ways of restoring our emotional and psychological energy. The psychiatrist Anthony Storr set out to explore why music has such a powerful effect on our minds and bodies. Drawing on a range of opinions, he suggests that the patterns of music make sense of our inner experience and give both structure and coherence to our emotions. At the end of his book, he concludes:

Music exalts life, enhances life, and gives it meaning. Great music outlives the individual who created it. It is both personal and beyond the personal. For those who love it, it remains a fixed point of reference in an unpredictable world. Music is a source of reconciliation, exhilaration, and hope which never fails. (Storr, 1992, p. 188)

Our loss of live music during the pandemic meant that for some it became possible to be restored by a virtual experience of music, rather as virtual contact with our fellow human beings via online platforms was a way of staying in touch with family, friends and colleagues.

The 'Serenade to Music' combined words and music. Words alone can be therapeutic, not only within a good experience of psychotherapy, when the naming of difficult feelings can enhance our capacity to bear them, but in the writing and reading of literature. It is possible to get lost both in the writing and the reading. A series of programmes about the writer Ernest Hemingway gave examples of both. When writing *A Farewell to Arms*, Hemingway was quoted as saying: 'I remember living in the book and making up what happened in it every day. Making the country and the people and the things that happened, I was happier than I had ever been' (BBC Four, *Hemingway, Part II*, 6 July 2021). This capacity to live in the book not only produced great literature but gave him respite from the turbulent nature of much of his life and personality. It could also cause friction in his relationships, for example with another writer, Martha Gellhorn:

> It is exactly as if he were dead or visiting on the moon. He writes and when he is through, he goes into a silence. He protects himself from anything and everything, takes no part in this world, cares about nothing, except what he is writing. He's about as much use as a stuffed squirrel, but he is turning out a beautiful story and nothing on earth besides matters to him. (BBC 4, *Hemingway, Part IV*, 20 July 2021)

However, it is not only the writer who can be absorbed in a creative way but also the reader. Abraham Verghese, a writer on Hemingway, commented:

I'm a big believer that, you know, the process of reading fiction is, the writer provides you some of the words, but you provide your imagination, and the great pleasure is, you're making this movie, and it's always striking how different our movies are as readers. (BBC Four, *Hemingway, Part III*, 13 July 2021)

This could be described as active participation, just as the members of a live audience at a concert are participating actively in the performance by being present, listening and applauding. Similarly, those involved in the making or appreciating of art are participating actively and practising what I call creative repair. Sometimes such engagement with the creative arts is affected by grief and/or trauma, so that being helped to express that grief is an important aspect of the other component of the concept of creative repair, what in psychoanalysis is known as the repair of the damaged object.

Repair of the damaged object

In order to appreciate the psychoanalytic understanding of the idea of the repair of the damaged object, it is necessary to know about the impact of early experience on each of us. The pioneering work with children of the psychoanalyst Melanie Klein is best approached via the later and more accessible psychoanalyst Donald Winnicott, who developed Kleinian thinking and is now cited more often in clinical circles than Klein herself. Reflecting on their work, it's as if when we come into the world we have to begin the *work* of existence. Whereas in the womb our cells just carried on multiplying and developing and we were fed automatically, after birth we have to breathe and suck and give voice to our needs. We are dependent on others to respond to our needs, and we go on developing and growing. Winnicott has written about the importance of the 'good-enough' mother who attends to her baby but does not anticipate her or his needs (Winnicott, 1964). It is a sort of dance in which she creates a safe place for her baby that is at first very intense, but gradually allows the baby to gain confidence in her or his own voice. It is the baby's task to 'train' the mother in how much she or he can take in so as not to be left under- or over-fed or stimulated. If the mother is preoccupied with her own problems or not interested in her baby, then this opportunity is lost and the feeding becomes mechanical and partial. This helps to explain how an early relationship can be damaged.

Whatever the circumstances, the baby's primary task is to survive, and we know from the work of John Bowlby (1979) that there is an instinct to attach to whoever or whatever is available in order to keep going. As babies we take in whatever there is, so that if, for example, our mother is depressed, we take in the symptoms of that depression. Nowadays neuroscience is confirming what we have known intuitively for centuries, namely that we need to be held and loved and accompanied as we begin to make sense of our experience (Gerhardt, 2004).

It will be clear thus far that a baby cannot itself influence the capacity of the mother to give him or her what is needed for emotional and psychological as well as physical survival. Sometimes there are other people around who can supplement what the primary carer cannot supply. These may be relatives or close family friends. The baby internalizes the experience of these primary relationships. Those sufficiently fortunate to have a good-enough internal object, that is to say, an experience of 'good-enough' parenting deep inside the psyche, go on to draw on that richness within and pass it on to others, whether actual children or others for whom they have a pastoral or other quasi-parental responsibility. For those who emerge from childhood or adolescence with an emotional deficit, there are various possibilities. Tragically, some may go on to pass on their experience of deprivation to another generation or do harm to others who come within their orbit. However, others seek out, whether consciously or unconsciously, alternative sources of emotional and psychological repair. This may come in the form of a good school experience or some youth group or important friendship.

It was Melanie Klein who pioneered child analysis in the 1930s and 1940s and wrote about 'the loss of the loved object' and the importance of 'making reparation to the object' (Klein, 1992, p. 265).[1] Here the word 'object' is not to be confused with an inanimate thing, but is meant as the object of the carer's affection, the baby loved by the carer, the carer being usually, but not always, the mother (see Chapter 6 for a discussion of the creative repair of some objects, as shown on the BBC's *The Repair Shop*). Klein applied and developed Freud's theory of the importance of two contrasting drives, a life drive that included the urge for self-preservation and a death drive, 'a force that strove to return the human being back into a state of inertia, of the inorganic' (Mitchell, 1998, p. 16). The human infant is born helpless and dependent on others for the satisfaction of its basic needs. 'Human beings bring something with them, but the mind's divisions are set up by the encounter with the world, with the commands, phantasies and wishes of others – with humankind's cultures, law and prohibitions' (Mitchell, 1998, pp. 18–19).

Klein built on Freud's theories and applied them to children. She argued that 'though there were differences in the mental apparatus of children and adults, the same psychoanalytic treatment could be applied to both' (Mitchell, 1998, p. 19). This applied to the thinking rather than the method, because she developed a 'play technique' for working with children. Having made available general play materials such as water, pencils and paper as well as toys such as small human figures, a train, a car etc., Klein observed and interpreted how the child dealt with the toys and the analytic space. By using this technique with very young and disturbed infants she developed insights into the earliest preverbal forms of communication, which informed her account of the phantasies and psychic contents of the neonatal and infantile mind.

Working with children and adults Klein developed a basic model of human development. The baby 'exists in relationship to another person or part of that person, prototypically the mother and the breast' (Mitchell, 1998, p. 21). In time the infant's world becomes more complex and includes the father or other co-parent. In order to survive a world which can be both satisfying and frustrating, the baby adopts a number of defences such as *splitting*, in which itself and the object are split off into a good part and a bad part, the badness being split off into the outside world. In time the baby is able to experience the mother as a whole object and wants to repair any damage done to her in phantasy.

The wish to repair damage done in past relationships may take several generations to come to fruition. All of us can reflect on our experience of growing up and standing, symbolically, on our parents' shoulders. I remember discussing this with a young man and asking him whether he thought that his parents had stood on their parents' shoulders and his swift reply was that they had done that twice over. This did not mean that he had no issues to be worked on, but that he respected the huge effort that his parents had made to give him and his brother more than they had received themselves. Many years ago, when working with a woman who had had a very difficult childhood spent mostly in care, I was curious about the way in which she had given her own children such a good experience. After a while, it emerged that there was a woman in the village who had invited her for tea quite regularly and had read to her. My client also loved nature, which had been a reliable source of comfort. She had drawn on this experience and also on her good relationship with an in-law who had always been very welcoming to her.

A good-enough experience of growing up not only impacts on the child but can also impact on any future generations. However, a good-enough experience of childhood is not the only factor affecting good internal objects. Whatever our experience of growing up, any of us can be vulnerable to a traumatic event at any point in our lives. Trauma can take many generations to be worked through, even though now-adays there are excellent sources of help for post-traumatic stress disorder (PTSD). It is interesting to reflect on the fact that many of the pioneers of the therapeutic professions were refugees from tyrannical regimes, perhaps trying to find ways of repairing themselves and others. So often this wish to repair is unconscious, especially when we do not actually know what our parents went through.

My own experience may be typical of that of many of the so-called baby boomers. As a post-war baby I grew up with a sister who had been three years old when the Second World War broke out and my father, an Anglican priest, joined the Royal Air Force as a chaplain. He spent four years away, three years in the Far East, so that he and my sister did not see one another for those four years. He and my mother wrote regularly to each other, but all letters were censored, so communication of deeper matters was limited. Sadly, when he returned, my sister did not recognize him and my father, whose childhood had been problematic and who had not had access to psychological insight, took offence and their relationship never quite recovered. I grew up oblivious of this but puzzled by the fact that my father would never talk of his experiences either of childhood and adolescence or of his time with the RAF. In such cases the trauma remains unconscious yet can be passed on to future generations.

In order to repair this unprocessed psychological damage, we may find our way into professions which may help us to do so. I now recognize that my unconscious attraction first to the study of history then, after the breakdown of my marriage, to training as a couple counsellor and group analyst was my ongoing attempt to make sense of this experience. This idea of unconscious attraction to reparative organizations has been highlighted by the group analyst Robin Skynner (Skynner, 1989). Writing of his experience of leading training and case-discussion groups, he discusses the importance of the practitioners' self-awareness if they are to grow professionally. Although he does not claim originality in observing that those in the helping professions are initially attracted to those roles by the need to solve their own problems, he adds that their experiences support the idea 'that people may become especially suited to the work they have unconsciously chosen, once they gain insight into their motivation' (Skynner, 1989, p. 11).[2]

I believe that this can be a serial progression if we change disciplines. Interpreting this personally, I 'chose' first to study then to teach history as a way of understanding my family's history and repairing my child self. Later, in training to be a couple counsellor, I understood the unconscious factors in the breakdown of my marriage. Later still, by training as a group analyst, I made sense of the social dynamics of having been brought up in a vicarage at a time when the house seemed to be an extension of the parish. Later still, after many fruitful years of analytical psychotherapy as a patient, both in groups and individually, I was free to explore a latent vocation to the priesthood, while still practising as a psychotherapist. Finally, via postgraduate studies in pastoral and practical theology, I have brought clinical and theological reflection together in naming and expanding this concept of creative repair.

The process of writing about it advances the integration of my life experience and thinking about the importance of repairing oneself via engaging in the creative arts. While study-ing I was encouraged to write a 'creative repair journal' to help record and reflect on my experience. Heather Walton has written about the value of writing, whether a journal or more structured life-writing: 'Journal writing has an immediacy, vividness and informality that may be lacking in other forms of reflective writing; sometimes the urgency of "getting something down" in the midst of challenging circumstances produces very fine writing indeed' (Walton, 2014, p. 45). This cathartic effect can be helpful when processing grief. However, sometimes, the act of writing can seem to be inaccessible. I referred earlier to examples of blocked creativity, perhaps as a result of buried grief. This merits further discussion.

Grief and creativity

As I indicated in Chapter 1, it was an experience of grief that led indirectly to the concept of creative repair. This was a result of reflecting on my father's experience while I was grieving the death of my former husband. This was part of the normal grieving process for me, although I recognized that I carry a lot of repressed grief from earlier generations. It is common in clinical work to meet people whose depression is the result of repressed or denied grief. In time the former losses are sufficiently grieved as to enable the initiation or resumption of creative projects that are brought to completion. If grief is blocked or denied, it is often experienced as depression, and our capacity to be creative is affected. Conversely, grief appropriately expressed can release creativity. Psychoanalytic, particularly Kleinian, theory has made an enormous contribution to our understanding of this. Klein, like Freud, wanted to explore why so many of our attempts to create something are sabotaged by our own tendency to destroy it. The graduate student I mentioned at the beginning of Chapter 1 suffered from this impulse to destroy what he had written.

Freud coined the expression 'death instinct' (Freud, 1984, p. 316)[3] to describe the instinct to return to the inanimate state (Freud, 1984, p. 311).[4] He contrasted this with 'the group of the sexual instincts' which are 'the true life instincts' and posed a conflict between them. The idea of the death instinct has been extended by Klein and her followers.[5] This builds on the topographical model of the mind which Freud developed and revised (Freud, 1984, 1923). It is useful to understand what Freud thought to be a model of the mind, because it has been the basis for later developments. He saw the mind as composed of the *Ego*, the *Super-ego* and the *Id*. The *Ego* is concerned with rational thinking, external perception and voluntary motor function or movement. It comprises mostly waking functions concerned with external reality and suspended in sleep. It is at the centre of our object relations, both as they are represented in our inner world and as they are met in the outer world. The *Ego* has to heed the *Super-ego*. The *Super-ego* is built up from internalized representations and standards of parental figures from infancy onwards. There may be contributions from relationships with teachers and other admired/feared figures. It can distinguish between more primitive and punitive aspects

('Thou shalt not...') and a more positive Ego-ideal or those precepts we may try to follow. This implies an interpersonal dimension that includes others in the external world who become internalized and set up as internal representations or images. Such images are not exact representations of real past external figures but, coloured by our feelings towards them, may become exaggeratedly good or bad objects. The *Id* is the basic biological aspect of the psyche, those inherited instinctual and constitutional aspects largely shared with other higher primates. Darwin wrote: 'Man with all his noble qualities ... still bears in his bodily frame the indelible stamp of his lowly origin' (Brown and Peddar, 1991, p. 47).

In Klein's development of the Freudian model, in order to survive the baby arbitrarily splits the world into *good* and *bad*. Bad or persecuting experiences are projected unconsciously into the breast, which is then itself experienced as persecuting. In the same way the libido is also projected into the breast, producing an ideal object in order to keep out the bad object which might otherwise annihilate both the ideal object and the self. This idea of the persecuted or idealized breast is part of Klein's pioneering work in understanding the baby's mind. It was drawn from careful observation of, and work with, children. In a seminal paper, after dealing with the mechanism of splitting as one of the earliest ways of defending against anxiety, Klein introduces the ideas of introjection and projection. As the infant develops, it introjects (or takes inside) the complete object, that is to say that the loved and hated aspects of the mother are no longer felt to be so widely separated, resulting 'in an increased fear of loss, states akin to mourning and a strong feeling of guilt, because the aggressive impulses are felt to be directed against the loved object. The depressive position has come to the fore' (Klein, 1975 (1946–63), p. 14). For Kleinian psychoanalyst Hannah Segal, the depressive position is absolutely crucial to the creative process. In the depressive position the whole object is loved and introjected and forms the core of an integrated ego. However, the infant has to cope with a new anxiety – fear of the loss of the loved object in the external world and his own inside. Greedy and sadistic impulses still hold sway attacking the loved object. Segal states,

> The memory of the good situation, when the infant's ego contained the whole loved object, and the realisation that it has been lost through his own attacks, gives rise to an intense feeling of loss and guilt, and to the wish to restore and re-create the loved object outside and within the ego. This wish to restore is the basis of later sublimation and creativity. (Segal in Klein, Heimann and Money-Kyrle, 1955, p. 386)

In other words, it is the recognition of our aggressive potential that provokes the creative wish to make things better. Encountering loss and guilt are directly connected with creativity. But what of those who split off that sense of loss and guilt? Might they suffer from blocked creativity? Later in the same paper Segal points to an explanation for creative block:

> If the wish to create is rooted in the depressive position and the capacity to create depends on a successful working through it, it would follow that the inability to acknowledge and overcome depressive anxiety must lead to inhibitions in artistic expression. (Segal in Klein, Heimann and Money-Kyrle, 1955, p. 390)

Hannah Segal goes on to give a clinical example of a patient, a young girl with a definite gift for painting. After some analysis she started to paint again but did decorative handicraft work in preference to 'real painting', denying that it mattered to her. She was unable to acknowledge her depression about the wounding and depression of her father. The dream that revealed this also revealed the impact of denial of depression on her painting.

> In relation to her painting the denial of the depth and seriousness of her depressive feelings produced the effect of superficiality and prettiness in whatever she chose to do—the dead father is denied and no ugliness or conflict is ever allowed

to disturb the neat and correct form of her work. (Segal in Klein, Heimann and Money-Kyrle, 1955, p. 391)

This recognition that denial of depression blocks creativity has also informed much of my own clinical work, particularly that which has focused on the creative block of writers or university researchers. Some time ago, I had an interesting conversation with a poet and photographer, who was happy for me to cite his experience anonymously. In an email, he described suffering a period of ME-type illness during which his mother became chronically ill and fell into a coma. Having regretted not being at his father's deathbed some years earlier, he wanted to be with his dying mother. His own words describe the impact of this:

> It's an incredible experience to watch the process of death so closely. This had a huge impact on me and still does. It made me realise that our time is short and being alive is a precious thing full of potential. It really kick-started me again to GET ON WITH IT! Don't waste time. I'd been toying with putting a ... book together for some while and now I set myself the target of the anniversary of my mum's death. I was on course but a few technical hitches held me up. Nevertheless I was only five weeks overdue ... I'm now working on my seventh tome and have had several exhibitions of my photos.

This moving account of the close correlation between acknowledged grief (and the wish to put something right with the second parent) and released creativity does, I hope, give flesh to the technical language of the Kleinian theory.

Conclusion

By now it should be clear that the concept of creative repair has been evolving for some years. It brings together the importance of the creative arts as a vital source and resource for all who routinely expend their emotional and psychological energy in the service of others and the importance of repairing damage to the internal world done by poor early experience or later damage to the healthy ego due to the experience of trauma. During the recent pandemic the concept has been affirmed by the many accounts of emotional and psychological deprivation caused by the cessation of live performances whether professional or amateur. Whether we are involved in reading or writing, music or art, as performative participants or as recipients of the creativity of others, we bring our imagination to our experiences in order to make them our own. I would argue that the creative arts are an essential aspect of the well-being of us all, but for those of us who work with others in a context of pastoral care, broadly interpreted, they are vital if we are to avoid exhaustion or even burnout.

Notes

1 Although Klein's original writings can be hard to understand, perhaps, as with Freud, because English was for her a second language, Juliet Mitchell's summary chapter is very helpful (1998).

2 In a conversation with Robin Skynner on July 12th, 1991, I spoke of this and said that it was hard to accept one's unconscious motivation for entering professions that we believed we had chosen consciously, and his reply was that we could be very good at what we have 'chosen' to do.

3 Freud tried to make sense of the manifestations of a compulsion to repeat (which) exhibit to a high degree an instinctual character and when they act in opposition to the pleasure principle, give the appearance of some 'daemonic' force at work (Freud, 1984, p. 307).

4 An example of this might be that when someone suffering from clinical depression is in the grip of a depressive episode, there may be a strong pull to end life, or a longing for oblivion, in order to stop the pain.

5 Hannah Segal writes of the deflection of the death instinct, described by Freud, as consisting, in Melanie Klein's view, partly a projection, partly of the conversion of the death instinct into aggression. The ego splits itself and projects that part of itself which contains the death instinct outwards into the original external object – the breast. Thus the breast, which is felt to contain a great part of the infant death instinct, is felt to be bad and threatening to the ego, giving rise to a feeling of persecution (Segal, 1973, p. 25).

3

Why Self-care?

There are many people working in a variety of settings who are
routinely offering pastoral care or other ways of helping. How
are they to make sure that they do not suffer from accumulative
exhaustion or compassion fatigue? Many professions have
strategies built into their professional context. Counsellors and
psychotherapists are duty-bound to be in regular supervision.
They must also undertake Continuing Professional Development (CPD) by attending training and other events fulfilling
requirements that ensure that practitioners continue to reflect
on their experience and gain additional training and insight.
Those working in the NHS mental health services often have
access to reflective practice groups that offer some support for
their work. Counsellors and psychotherapists are advised to
take substantial clinical breaks in order both to restore their
own energy and to give their clients an opportunity to develop
their own inner resources as preparation for the end of the
therapy.

Pastoral care in a Christian context has been described as
'one in which concern and practical action for others – and
each other – is rooted in a common love of Christ' (Rose, 2013,
p. 3). While this can be very rewarding, it can also be draining,
and pastoral carers need to find ways of resourcing themselves.
Churches vary in their recognition of the importance of pastoral
supervision. It is obligatory for presbyters in the Methodist
Church. In the Anglican Church it may be encouraged but
not provided. Clergy are expected to find their own ways of
refreshing their ministry and reflecting on the impact of their
work on their emotional and psychological health. However,

dioceses are increasingly mindful of the need for Continuing Ministerial Development (CMD) and the importance of flourishing in ministry. Well-being and resilience have become key words in this context. Clergy are encouraged to take time for quiet days or a retreat to refresh their spiritual resources. Unlike most experiences of therapy, pastoral relationships are ongoing, so that ministry can seem to be never-ending. Appropriate self-care is essential if exhaustion and burnout are to be avoided. Many clergy function effectively for many years, so that an experience of exhaustion that is not the usual periodic fatigue, with recovery a matter of a holiday or retreat, is often a surprise and can affect self-esteem and confidence. Carol, for example, just managed to avoid burnout.

Carol

Carol had been in ministry for about eight years. As a curate, her Training Incumbent (TI) had been a hard-working priest who had moved from an inner-city parish to a rural benefice with seven churches. His model for ministry was one of being ever busy, so that Carol was expected to do the same. As she was required to continue post-ordination training, study time was built into her working agreement. This gave her the opportunity to compare notes with colleagues and enabled her to negotiate with her TI her need to develop a more paced approach to ministry. His 'I'm in charge' approach to ministry also meant that his expectations of his curate were limited, and he was not particularly interested in the development of her skills and competence. Carol completed her curacy successfully, although she lacked substantial experience of taking the Occasional Offices, having only officiated on her own at one or two baptisms, marriages and funerals, usually when her incumbent was on holiday.

She moved on to the role of Associate Priest in a team ministry in a country town and was able to expand her experience as part of a well-functioning team. It was then time to apply for her own incumbency post and she was successful in being appointed to a rural benefice with three churches for which she was their vicar. At first all went well. As there had been an interregnum of over a year, members of all three churches were relieved to have a vicar again. Anxious to please, Carol unwittingly reverted to the model to which she had been exposed in her curacy. She rushed around from church to church, chairing Parochial Church Council (PCC) meetings and trying to respond to all liturgical expectations and pastoral requests. Parishioners who had stepped up to help during the vacancy were happy to revert to a passive role. After a year of this, Carol was exhausted and disillusioned and during her first Ministerial Development Review (MDR), an annual opportunity to reflect on her ministry, admitted that she was close to burnout. With her reviewer she worked out a strategy to reduce the expectations she had of herself, and which others now had of her. Caught in time, Carol avoided burnout and consulted her spiritual director in order to follow through the changes needed as a result of her conversation with the MDR reviewer.

Reflection

1. Institutional flaws

There are various ways in which Carol had been let down by the Church as an institution. First, her ministry training course had given her lots of practical advice about taking services of all sorts, preaching and pastoral care. However, it had not helped her to think about the nature of pastoral relationships in which there was an imbalance of power. It did not give her a way of thinking about the vulnerability of those in new posts and the need to manage her expectations of herself and other people's expectations of her.

Second, although her sending diocese had been a pioneer in the development of training for new Training Incumbents, there was no curacy available for her there, so she was released to another diocese. There were no established and rigorous systems in place there for teaching new Training Incumbents in the skilful management of the relationship between incumbent and curate.

Third, when Carol came to apply for her own incumbency in the same diocese, the interviewers did not consider her need to replenish her resources. The previous incumbent had retired through illness, so that the opportunity to welcome a younger incumbent masked some of the difficult dynamics of the benefice.

2. *Personal shortcomings of the Training Incumbent*

Although there was some training for Training Incumbents, Carol's TI had not found the time to attend, so was repeating his own experience of curacy, in which the 'I'm in charge' vicar modelled overwork and a sense of being indispensable. One writer who has challenged this model of ministry is Andy Griffiths, who has reflected on his daughter's need to invent an imaginary father because she saw so little of him (2018, p. 4). The idea of reflecting on experience had not been part of the training of Carol's TI. As he had invested much of his identity in his ministerial role, he was wary of life without his clerical collar and took time off only when his wife organized family holidays. She insisted on infrequent breaks from parish life, and he was happy to oblige. His family provided the check and balance against exhaustion. Lacking self-awareness, he thought that his was the right way to practise ministry and had no insight into the power imbalance between himself and his curate that might have inhibited her capacity to challenge his way of doing things.

3. *Things for Carol to learn from her part in the experience*

Although Carol's ministerial training had included theological reflection, she had not been warned of the importance of regular self-reflection and attention to her emotional and psychological resources. Her post-ordination training and need for study time had protected her from fatigue during her curacy and the presence of the ministry team in her next post as Associate Priest had contributed to a false sense of security. She was unaware of the particular dangers of beginnings, in which the desire to please can obscure the need for a paced introduction to a new setting. In time, her spiritual director was able to support her in establishing new patterns in her daily life, which acted as a prophylactic protection from future exhaustion. Had she had the opportunity to develop healthy habits during ministry training, some of her future stress might have been avoided. This raises the issue of the importance of the quality of ministry training.

Initial ministerial education

Initial ministerial education has a vital role to play in the formation of healthy habits in the foundation of a person's ministry. In the previous chapter, I indicated the importance of our childhood template and here I want to consider its impact on new beginnings in later life. One of the important insights of psychoanalysis is the correlation between a sound emotional start in life and our capacity to manage other beginnings.[1] For each one of us any important beginning echoes, at an unconscious level, our very entry into the world at birth. This can range from school experiences and any new job or training experience to any new relationship or friendship. All beginnings have the power to stir up, albeit unconsciously, our experience of our entry into the world and subsequent childhood experience. If we are fortunate, we will have internalized a good-enough experience in our early life. If we have been left with an emotional deficit, then we may try to fill that internal space with addictive behaviours, which can include overactivity. Whatever the situation, we are likely to connect with anxiety in any important new experience. For example, in a therapeutic context it is usual for people to feel very anxious at the initial session, and it is the task of the counsellor to put the person at ease. When conducting an experiential group for the first time, it is to be expected that the group analyst will be aware of multiple anxieties coming through from the group members and this may be somatized in the form of a headache or other form of physical stress. A newly trained counsellor or group analyst will also be dealing with her or his anxiety about the new role. With good supervision this can be managed, especially because any clinician who has undergone a rigorous training will have been in therapy and be aware of their own particular vulnerabilities.

When it comes to clergy, the focus of their training is their future ministry after ordination. In her monograph *Training God's Spies*, Anne Tomlinson reflects on her experience of training candidates for lay and ordained ministry in the Scottish Church's Theological Institute. She deplores the 'culture of expediency' that sets in soon after the beginning of the three-year course. Reading becomes directed to the next assignment, rather than 'being a glorious trawl through the uncharted waters of different theological approaches' (Tomlinson, 2001, p. 3). A culture of busyness was already established in training and Tomlinson's attempts to persuade candidates to build more leisure into their schedules met with responses such as 'There'll be time for that once I've finished the course.' As will be already clear from Carol's experience, such an expectation is unlikely to be fulfilled in practice.

Training will probably include practice in listening skills and theological reflection; while valuable in themselves, these may stir up difficult feelings or memories for ordinands. Some courses allow for this and offer chaplaincy support for those being trained. Occasionally, professional counselling will be offered and funded, either by the course administration or the sending diocese. Some training includes a course in pastoral psychology which may or may not cover teaching about the unconscious. It is not routine, so that ordinands may be unaware of the impact of the past on the present. Not only childhood templates, but templates of previously known clergy may have a profound impact on the formation of future clergy.

In her study of a group of Anglican ordinands, Amanda Bloor explored how they assessed what it might mean to 'put on' priesthood. Her long-term research project revealed that many of them measured their vocation not against theory or theology, but against the example of priests they had known and admired. This was the case whether they came from evangelical or more catholic backgrounds. She writes: 'Whatever the underlying theology, it was the attractiveness of the example provided by particular priests that drove aspiring clergy to consider ordination. The individuals they had observed became templates of what dedicating oneself to Christian service could involve' (Bloor, 2013, p. 19). Bloor found that these idealized views of ministry were not usually modified during the formation process. This indicates that unless the course offers a specific and intentional focus on the need to establish healthy habits that support the restoration of energy used in ministry, ordinands are likely to revert to their internalized past experience of clergy or – as in Carol's case – be exposed to the practice and role model of their Training Incumbent.

Whereas trainee counsellors are required to have an experience of therapy as part of their training, those training for ministry are not required to have had such an experience and so may not be aware of the unconscious factors that can emerge in later beginnings. Carol's Training Incumbent had not allowed himself any opportunity to think about offering something for Carol that met her needs rather than his own need to repeat his own experience. Nor had his own ministerial training encouraged him to develop new habits and establish healthy patterns which could later stand candidates in good stead when they moved on to their first ministry posts. This meant that he was passing on a model of ministry, perhaps the template of a previous vicar he had known, that was centred around the person of the vicar. Thus in order to keep everything going, he rushed around taking services, failing to build up the strengths of others who worshipped with him. In his role as Training Incumbent, he had an opportunity to think again about how to model healthy patterns of ministry for Carol. This opportunity was missed. For her part, although Carol was aware of the mismatch between her TI's way of working and her needs for a more balanced approach, and did indeed discuss it with her post-ordination tutor, her choices were limited. It didn't quite equate to bullying, because her TI was understanding of her need for time out to study, so that a formal complaint did not seem appropriate. As the one with less power than her incumbent Carol felt vulnerable and, because she needed a favourable report from him in order to progress, she decided to weather her time as curate, knowing that in her next appointment she would actively seek the opportunity to be part of a ministry team. This raises the question of why her later experience seemed to be eclipsed by her experience of her curacy, which brings us to the importance of beginnings in ministry itself.

The importance of beginnings in ministry and the compulsion to repeat bad habits

As indicated earlier, beginnings are very powerful and unless we are taught to protect them from deeper unhealthy habits, the need to please and establish a reputation for hard work and enthusiastic ministry may set new ministers up for unrealistic patterns of worship, mission and pastoral care. In Carol's case, she reverted to the pattern to which she had been exposed in her curacy, even though, at a conscious level, she knew that it did not work for her. This compulsion to repeat is largely unconscious and worth explaining.

It was Freud who recognized the compulsion to repeat dysfunctional habits that can sabotage our creative intentions. He formulated a structure of the mind through which aspects of our conscious and unconscious behaviour could be understood as inter-related. I summarized this in Chapter 2 (p. 23). Whereas the Ego can be thought of as the rational part of our mind which acts as a mediator between the demands of the outer world and the needs of the inner world, it must take account of the Super-ego, the 'should' voice coming from inner parental voices from the past. Amanda Bloor's research demonstrates the impact of previously known influential clergy or other leaders on the ordinands' expectations of themselves in future ministry (2013). Meanwhile the Id, the basic biological aspect of the psyche, is the more primitive aspect of our mind and explains the tendency for fight or flight when under pressure or in an emergency. When we are stressed or anxious, we tend to retreat into our more primitive selves.

When we begin a new job, relationship or role, our childhood template can influence how we manage our anxiety while we settle into the new experience. Past experiences may come to our aid, but in the case of Carol and her ministry experience, although during her time as an Associate Priest as part of a well-functioning ministry team she had to some extent repaired the curacy experience of being shown a model of overwork, when it was her turn to become an incumbent, the model of her own Training Incumbent came to the fore. It was an unconscious reversion to her curacy experience, only this time it was the internalized behaviour of her incumbent which, combined with her own anxiety to please and the need of the parishioners to have a parental figure back in charge, directed her patterns of ministry. These patterns were unsustainable, so that it was only a matter of time before she became exhausted. Thanks to the well-timed Ministerial Development Review and subsequent support from her spiritual director, Carol was able to negotiate a new way of balancing the ministerial tasks that drained her with regular ways of restoring her emotional and psychological energy. Such change needs to be intentional and externally supported, because it is difficult to replace former, internalized models of behaviour.

The role of creative repair in the formation of good habits during training or at any new beginning

While the formation of new habits at any time will be considered more extensively in later chapters, especially Chapter 7, there is a particular benefit in this being part of ministry training and, by extension, any new beginning. If we accept that our childhood template influences other beginnings, then it follows that beginnings mean that we revert to early templates. The time of ministry training is, potentially, an ideal time to develop new habits and establish healthy patterns that could later stand candidates in good stead when they move on to their first ministry posts. Engagement in creative repair during ministry formation could help to do this. For it to take place with integrity, it would be important for staff tutors to model good practice and establish sound structures for not over-working. Anecdotally, various tutors have indicated that this is not necessarily the case. They, too, have been brought up in the culture of over-busyness. When researching into the possibility of developing sustainable healthy patterns of life and ministry, two members of a focus group who were involved in the training of Anglican ordinands commented on the difficulty in persuading students to take time off to engage in creative pursuits. This echoes Tomlinson's experience. Having bemoaned the lost opportunity for training candidates to build more leisure into their schedules, she went on to make a theological case for the crucial role of the imagination, writing: 'It is my contention that the action of the Spirit – this power that makes connections between the extraordinary and the ordinary in our lives, that rouses us into being aware of the Infinite in the finite – is identical to that of the imagination; that the imagination, in other words, is the spark of the Spirit' (Tomlinson, 2001, p. 17). While I might take issue with Tomlinson's pneumatology,[2] her passion for the inclusion of creativity in the formation process resonates with my own thinking about the importance of creative repair.

In order to change this situation, either current tutors or

current trainees would need to be convinced of the importance of a prophylactic approach to the avoidance of burnout. Given the vulnerability of ordinands, who are usually appropriately anxious at the beginning of their training, it is more likely that tutors would be pioneers in this trans-generational shift in attitude. If they can be persuaded to regard ongoing self-care as an essential ingredient in all ministry, they could influence future generations.

From time to time, when invited to do so, I have given a session on the practice of creative repair to groups of Anglican ordinands or new curates, in more than one diocese. In order to demonstrate the possibility of engaging in a short creative repair experience, I have found the following exercise useful. Having invited the group to refrain from talking, I have played a piece of reflective sacred music lasting for about seven minutes, during which time they were free to stay in their places or wander round the room looking at various pictures or artworks set up earlier. The intention was that they would lose themselves in the task, whether in the music, the break from speech, or in looking at the art. Afterwards, I would give them time to re-enter the world of speech and invite them to reflect on their experience. The mood of the group would have changed from a discursive space to one of reflection and most would articulate the value of the experience, like a mini quiet time. The fact that they were attending the session as part of training seemed to give them permission to enter into this experience. However, during a general discussion later, certain group members would comment that they would be unlikely to be able to do this away from the training.

On one occasion, I was told by an ordinand that the combination of the need to earn a living, the demands of the part-time course and their ongoing roles in their churches meant that there was very little time for such an activity. Yet for many of them there would be time for physical exercise. I suggested that the needs of the soul were complementary to the needs of the body and that I had just demonstrated how much could be experienced in a few minutes of dedicated time. On another occasion, a curate spoke to me afterwards and indicated the need to educate churchwardens and congregations if the importance of creative repair was to be acknowledged. She gave the example of her husband, the vicar, who would paint a picture on his day off, but if a parishioner came to the door would feel guilty about being caught in such an act of creativity. However, the session had been useful in giving some authority to his activity and she agreed that there was work to be done in educating parishioners not to come to the door on his day off unless there was a genuine emergency.

Turning around generations of professional habits of excessive busyness is not easy. Negotiating any modification of dysfunctional patterns of behaviour is often a struggle. Within a psychotherapy context, I compare the desire for and negotiation of change to be rather like turning a tanker round in a narrow stretch of water. The decision to engage in therapy is an important first step. Having established a safe enough therapeutic relationship in which I can be trusted to support or challenge without intrusiveness, the work can begin. Next comes an exploration of the person's family history, childhood template and a recognition of any emotional or psychological deficiencies either from early life or from later, adult experiences. As part of the ongoing work, I usually invite people to reflect on what resources them and what drains them. In order for this to be useful, they need to try to suspend all expectations and adopt a position of curiosity, observing how they feel after a variety of events or activities. There are often several surprises. Although theirs is an informal audit (see Appendix B) rather than a questionnaire, I invite you to complete one at some point before moving on to the next chapter. As an example, this was the result of Frank's informal audit.

Frank

Frank had been working as a hospital doctor for about 15 years. He had entered medicine full of enthusiasm and determined to make a difference. He became a specialist in respiratory illness and a consultant with a reputation for competence and had a friendly manner which was appreciated by his patients. He has been a Christian since medical school and attended his local church when he could. He was the lead author in a number of research papers and enjoyed working collaboratively with other specialists in his field. Happily married with one child, his life seemed enviable to his friends and colleagues. This was until the onset of the Covid pandemic. Given his specialism, he was much in demand and the number of admissions to his ward and subsequent deaths during the first wave of the virus began to overwhelm his usual capacity to sustain his work. His wife contracted the virus and although she was not hospitalized, she has suffered from long Covid. Frank did not catch it but had to self-isolate for some of the time. His usual resilience faded, his mood became uncharacteristically low, and his GP recommended counselling for support.

Initial sessions revealed that Frank had grown up in a single-parent family, brought up by a devoted father after his mother had died of pneumonia not long after giving birth to his younger brother Tim. His maternal grandparents had helped out when they could, although there seemed to be some rivalry between them and his father regarding the care of Frank and Tim. His father had not remarried and was now a devoted grandfather to Frank's daughter, the first girl in his family for several generations. As we explored his background, I commented to Frank on the lack of robust female figures in his life. He recognized that he had been coping relatively well with the pandemic and extra shifts but that his morale sagged when his wife Linda became ill. Although not trained in psychology, he could see the connection between Linda's protracted illness and the loss of his own mother to pneumonia when he was four years old. He was also curious about his unconscious longing to repair his mother's illness by specializing in respiratory diseases. As Robin Skynner had put it, such information did not stop him from being good at what he had 'chosen' to do (Skynner, 1989, p. 11; see Chapter 2, note 2). He was keen to rediscover his enthusiasm for his work. Although his GP had wondered about medication, they had agreed that it would be worth trying counselling first.

After a few sessions, in which he seemed to benefit from the focused attention which I as a quasi-mother-figure was able to offer, I asked Frank how he usually resourced himself, given the demands of his job even in pre-Covid times. His immediate response was that his home life meant everything to him, as well as his Christian faith. As a keen cricketer, he tried to keep fit out of season by going to the gym. As the pandemic had impacted all of these regular activities, including church attendance, I invited him to notice what now resourced him and what drained him over the period of a fortnight. I asked him to approach it without any assumptions about what should or should not be expected to resource him. As he was unable to attend the following week, he welcomed this task as a link to our work.

Two weeks later he returned and seemed puzzled. As the restrictions had eased, he had been able to return to the gym and had expected that this would resource him. From a physical point of view his body felt better for the exercise, but he returned home emotionally drained. Conversely, as his wife Linda was still quite unwell, he had taken on cooking the family evening meal and had expected this to be a drain on his resources. Although he had found it a challenge to look up recipes and ask Linda for hints about making various dishes, he had found this new role very resourcing. Their daughter, now seven years old, had wanted to help him and the whole family, including his father when he was invited to join them, were delighted with the results. At his wife's suggestion he had begun to try drawing and found that his surgeon's dexterity helped him to get started. As he reported all this, he became quite animated. We reflected on his findings and began to speculate about the disappointing experience of the gym. I encouraged him to continue the process of noticing the impact of his activities on his mood and morale.

Reflection

This reflection combines both our joint reflection on Frank's experience and my later interpretation of some of his observations. At the beginning of our work, it was a relief for Frank to get off his chest how exhausted he was by the pandemic and its impact on him and his colleagues at work. He was just about coping with that until his wife contracted the virus and then developed long Covid. As we talked through the impact of overload, the various deaths and the sorrow of relatives, he realized that it was a combination of factors that had led to his low mood. While his home life had offered solace, despite the need to home-school his daughter, it was his wife's illness that had tipped the balance into feeling both overwhelmed and powerless to make people better. As a doctor, the need to save life was wired into his professional persona. Although he accepted that some people would die of respiratory diseases in pre-pandemic times, most of the time he was able to help his patients to extend their expected lifespan. Colleagues were going through similar experiences, so that he knew that he was not alone professionally. However, unconscious fears of losing his wife and thus repeating his father's experience of becoming a single parent were a factor unique to his own experience. Once this was recognized, Frank was able to understand why he felt so much worse than his colleagues, stretched though they all were. This recognition helped to make sense of things and his mood began to lift, which gave him the mental space to be able to observe what resourced and what drained him.

We considered Frank's surprise at his experience when he was able to return to the gym, and discussing this in greater detail it emerged that the sight of other people exercising, often puffing and panting, kept reminding him of those he treated in hospital, who fought for every breath even if they recovered eventually thanks to intensive care. I suggested that this was what I often refer to as a 'trauma trace', when something in the here and now connects with a previous traumatic experience and thus provokes a stronger reaction than the event itself would usually provoke. As a temporary measure, we considered other forms of exercise, so that he began to take up running instead. His local swimming pool was not yet open, but he could consider that later. Later, as the pandemic eased and he felt better resourced, he returned to the gym with reduced expectations of how he would feel afterwards.

The need to take over cooking for the family prompted Frank to enter new territory and at first his lack of confidence made it quite stressful. However, encouraged by his family and inspired by the enthusiasm of his daughter, he both enjoyed their shared activity and began to realize that he could move beyond the basics and experiment a little. This creativity was a first experience of creative repair. Further, his past experience of seeing his father cope when he was a child meant that he had an internal role model of a father cooking for his family. As his father had recently had an early diagnosis of Parkinson's disease, his dexterity was now limited, so he really looked forward to joining the family at weekends. As Frank's wife Linda began to recover to some extent, she helped when she could, so that together they worked as a team. Looking at this through a group-analytic lens, the family group was more than the sum of its parts. (This is a key concept in group analysis. See Chapter 5 for an explanation of the value of group process.)

Finally, Frank's wife had always suspected that he would be able to draw if he applied himself. As a present to thank him for his efforts in the kitchen, she bought him a sketch pad, various pencils and a subscription to an online drawing course. He was very touched by this and was determined to put in the effort to justify this gift. Unsurprisingly, his surgeon's dexterity and careful attention to detail gave him a head start in learning how to draw. I encouraged him to set regular time aside around his shifts in order to consolidate this new hobby, which used a different part of his brain and enabled him to see the world through fresh eyes. This was his second experience of creative repair.

Frank did raise the impact of the pandemic and the many deaths on his Christian faith. As he knew me only as a therapist, I did not respond to this as a priest but listened to his doubts and thought with him about a possible discussion with one of the ministers in his church whom he had found reflective about the relation between faith and suffering. Without prompting from me, he began to see that being creative was a way of accessing God as Creator, and that while there was no denying his struggle at work, at home he felt loved and encouraged to resource himself through his newly discovered creativity.

I realize that at an unconscious level Frank would have internalized our work and me as someone who affirmed his willingness to broaden his approach to the need to resource himself routinely if he were to sustain the demanding nature of his specialist discipline. In time these new habits and the ongoing good relationship with his wife meant that he could bring the sessions to an end. Therapists are usually working to make themselves redundant, a practice which is not paralleled in the same way in pastoral care. A pastor is always there unless she or he moves to another church setting, so that exact comparisons are not appropriate. However, boundaries are important in pastoral care if the pastor is not to suffer from burnout. While they are not as precise as those of a therapeutic setting, mindful pastors can take care not to offer longer or more frequent meetings than can be reasonably sustained over time.

Conclusion

While the experiences of both Carol and Frank reflect the respective challenges of different professional settings, each has a dedicated working life of service to or care of others. In each case they were taken aback by their exhaustion and dangerously close contact with burnout. Similar professions in which there is no built-in strategy for self-care include other areas of medicine, teachers at all levels of education and those providing nursing or social care. For Carol, the annual MDR came just in time to prevent a complete breakdown and her spiritual director picked up the baton from the MDR reviewer, so that she established new rhythms in order to sustain her ongoing ministry. In Frank's case, the experience of psychodynamic counselling in which he uncovered unconscious factors in his collapse of morale helped him to make sense of his experience. Having begun to feel better, his discovery of untapped creative potential both in the kitchen and in his drawing gave him a new sense of purpose. Not only did he have new strategies for sustaining his demanding medical practice, but he avoided realizing his unconscious fear of repeating his father's experience of single parenting.

Whereas the experience of Carol highlighted the need for more sustainable habits in ministry, that of Frank introduced the potential of creative repair to restore his energy and morale in a sustainable way. These twin themes of the importance of changing habits and the value of introducing creative repair will be developed in future chapters.

Notes

1 The general importance of life stages was first considered within psychoanalysis by Freud and has been developed by others, especially Erikson (1950) and Jacobs (1986) among others.

2 Her easy equation between the imagination and the work of the Holy Spirit is perhaps an example of exaggeration to make a point. As John V. Taylor (1972) suggested in his pioneering examination of the work of the Holy Spirit, with his idea of the Go-Between God, the third person of the Trinity allows for communication in the here and now. Perhaps a more apt reference to the Trinity within the creative arts is to be found in *The Mind of the Maker* (1994) in which Dorothy L. Sayers made a comparison between the Trinity and the process of writing.

4

Individual Creative Repair

Creative repair can be practised individually or with others. Originally, I was concerned about the levels of stress among clergy and other care givers and focused on the prevention of burnout. Although, for the purposes of my research, creative repair involved engaging with the creative arts, it should not be restricted to that. Many other activities such as gardening, cooking, walking, listening to the radio or watching television or YouTube and other virtual access points can resource us. What matters is the impact of the activity on our bodily, psychological, or spiritual health. In this chapter I am drawing on past research in order to evidence my understanding of the value of creative repair in practice.

I shall be considering two different phases of research, each of which involved a focus group. For the first one, I invited a group of clergy to join an initial recorded focus group. It was a purposive sample of clergy from different traditions within the Church of England. Others who were unable to attend the face-to-face focus group were invited to complete a questionnaire (see Appendix A). Some important themes emerged from both the face-to-face and email groups. The second focus group took place later in the research process. Again, it was a purposive sample of clergy who were invited to take part in a recorded discussion. Important themes emerged.

Findings from the focus groups

The first theme to emerge was the real danger of burnout and the need to have healthy habits in place in order to prevent it. Two of the first focus group had experienced burnout and two more had come very close to it. One of them had taken up a craft activity that became a lifeline, because 'there was an area in me that was all kind of broken down and needed to be picked up again and made whole by this activity'. All of them identified the role of the creative arts either in the healing process or in the avoidance of burnout. Each highlighted the importance of continuing these practices in the prevention of any future crisis and would have valued a prophylactic approach which had prioritized these needs. Although Jenny was not a member of either group, her experience illustrates the dangers of burnout.

Jenny

Jenny had been a pastoral carer for many years as a lay leader before being ordained in the mid-1990s. A widow with two grown-up children and three small grandchildren, she had welcomed ministry as if it replaced her marriage and enjoyed working long hours. After becoming a grandmother, she wanted to support her daughters and spend quality time with each of them and their young children. However, she did not want to let down the many parishioners who had come to depend on her, so continued the weekly visits to them. She assumed that she could fit everything in, and that being with her family on her day off would resource her as it was such a positive experience, so that she failed to notice that fatigue was creeping up on her. It was only when a colleague noticed that she was nodding off in team meetings that Jenny acknowledged that even positive experiences can be exhausting.

Her vicar came to see her and encouraged her to talk through her weekly appointments. He recommended that she took time to plan a break which did not involve looking after small children. He also proposed a training session for the ministry team in which they would review their pastoral practice. As it had been so obvious that Jenny loved her work, the fatigue had been masked until it leaked into the meetings. Jenny took his advice and went on holiday with a friend. While away, she talked through what had happened and realized that her commitment to 'going the extra mile' was wearing her down. She made an appointment to see a spiritual director and asked her friend to keep an eye on her as she went back to work.

Reflection

It is often thought that any positive experience must *ipso facto* resource us. However, any changes, even changes for the better, can be stressful and need time for adjustment. Although Jenny seemed able to sustain her weekly pastoral visits even after the arrival of her grandchildren, she did not acknowledge that there was a limit to her emotional and psychological energy. By setting aside her days off for visiting and helping to care for her grandchildren, she failed to consider her other restorative needs. She might have examined whether she needed to go on with the weekly visits to her parishioners or whether she could space out her visits and help them to find other sources of care. Not only would this reduce their dependency on Jenny, but it would weaken what might have become a habit of co-dependency. One of the dangers of Christian pastoral care is the prevalence of phrases such as 'going the extra mile', drawn from the biblical story of the Good Samaritan (Luke 10.25–37). What this well-meant habit fails to emphasize is that going the *extra* mile is not an *everyday* event. There are times when it is appropriate to do more than is required for a particular situation, but afterwards it is necessary to rebalance and put back the reserve resources which have been drawn upon for that situation.

At a deeper level, it is possible that Jenny's sense of identity and self-worth may be lodged in the care she gives to others. This sets her up to project her needs onto those of others and therefore to look after herself vicariously. This is common with many people who spend their time caring for others, whether professionally, like nurses or teachers, or voluntarily like some charity workers and many pastoral carers. It can lead to an experience of feeling exploited or taken for granted but can be avoided with healthy habits of work/life balance and sound boundaries. The need for boundaries in pastoral care was the second theme to emerge from the first focus group.

The complexity of boundaries in ministry

Whatever the textbooks may now recommend, it became clear that, in the experience of the focus group members, healthy boundaries were rarely modelled by those in senior roles. A culture of long hours and the need always to be busy contributed to fatigue, as did the failure to acknowledge the very demanding nature of pastoral care. Expectations of ministry do not help. As one commentator has put it, 'The standard expectation that ministry is a six-day-a-week role, often requiring long hours in the evening, is death-dealing' (Grosch-Miller, 2021, p. 152). Some of these aspects – the failure of those in senior roles to model healthy boundaries; the culture of long hours and the need always to be busy – are resonant of past approaches to pastoral care and speak to Jenny's experience.

In the work of psychotherapists and counsellors, the importance of boundaries is imprinted on trainees as they begin their course. Many of them will have been required to be in therapy both before and during training and that experience will already have taught them about boundaries – strict time boundaries such as beginning and ending the sessions on time, no personal disclosures by the counsellor, the counsellor being a stranger to the client, an assumption that the counsellor is in regular supervision and has had a rigorous training, and a knowledge that as clients they are being cared for responsibly. The ending of therapy is kept in mind from the beginning, in order to limit the client's dependency to the minimum required to facilitate trust in a productive therapeutic relationship. Counsellors are bound by the ethical framework of their professional bodies such as the British Association of Counselling and Psychotherapy (BACP) and the United Kingdom Council for Psychotherapy (UKCP), which also have procedures for any complaints from clients.

Pastoral care differs from counselling in various ways. The two parties usually know each other in a shared context, such as attendance at the same faith worship setting, or as a result of an encounter with one of the ministry team. Pastoral carers are usually good listeners and may have had some training in basic counselling skills, but will not have been required to be in therapy or even pastoral care themselves. Timings of meetings are likely to be less precise, although some limit is desirable and should be made clear. There is more scope for pastoral carers to share their own experience, although it is always worth considering whose needs are being met by such self-sharing. The boundaries of confidentiality need to be made clear, such as the need for permission to share concerns with other members of the pastoral team if appropriate. Now that there are better safeguarding procedures in place in most church settings, there is more understanding of the limits of confidentiality.

Unlike a counselling relationship, a pastoral relationship doesn't have an obvious ending unless one or other of the parties moves away. Ministry itself can seem unending and there are rarely obvious end results. As one person in the first focus group put it: 'A creative project ... has a beginning and an end: there is actually an end product to it and there is an end result. It's finished and you've got something as a result. So it provides all the kinds of things that ministry very rarely brings.' A healthy understanding of the need for boundaries in pastoral care is essential. One parish priest commented on the need to set clear boundaries around a day off and that the use of the answerphone helped in terms of modelling good practice:

> 'I just erect a firm boundary, don't listen to the answer-phone or send emails and say, "Listen folks, I don't listen on a Monday." It's more than that, it's not just a day off, it's trying to help one another ... to break out of that "I'm indispensable" [attitude] ... it strikes me as such an import-ant gift that we have to experience and to share with the world.'

Such habits help to educate parishioners in the need for clergy and other pastoral carers to look after their own needs as well as care for others.

In addition, the emotional demands of pastoral encounters need to be recognized. As Jessica Rose has commented:

> Pastoral carers also have needs and risk becoming over-involved with those that they help, often without noticing it is happening. To be part of someone's healing process can be a powerful draw and make it hard to hold on to one's own role. An over-close attachment is something we can easily fall into. (2013, p. 50)

There need to be checks and balances against this danger, even among those who are fairly self-aware. Supervision and accountability help to protect both parties and the practice of creative repair is an important way of replenishing resources poured out in such encounters. This was evidenced by the members of both focus groups.

The value of creative repair

Most of the participants of each focus group recognized that failure to give proper place to their involvement in the creative arts spelt danger to their health and energy levels. The conversations highlighted the importance of creative repair for the prevention and cure of stress leading to exhaustion or even burnout. For example, one person spoke of having had a close shave with burnout and being spared this by a three-month sabbatical. Part of this had 'involved intensive reading like I've not done for years and years ... and that was amazingly creative for me'. Having recovered, regular time for reading or going to the theatre or concerts had been put in the diary as a crucial means of maintaining the recovery.

In their examination of what it is about the creative arts that is so helpful, two categories emerged from the first focus group. The first was the importance of a *physical* engagement with the creative arts. The group were interested in the holistic implications of body-based creativity. The second category was a consideration of what counts as participation and what does not. This was clarified as involving *active* participation, as for example when being taken in imagination into another world in a book or a film.

Anyone who has watched the BBC's *Strictly Come Dancing* will be aware of the intense physical work necessary if a celebrity is to learn whichever dance is being rehearsed. While the high standards of such a series will be beyond most people, evidence of the importance of dancing has featured in the second focus group and could be represented by the experience of Michelle.

Michelle

Michelle had always loved to dance but after her marriage broke down lost interest because she associated it with the ballroom dance competitions that she and her former husband had enjoyed before they had children. Later, after some years as a single parent, Michelle felt called to explore ordained ministry. During her training she became friends with another ordinand who lived 30 miles away and they discovered a shared love of dancing. Her friend introduced her to a group of line dancers.

By the time of the focus group, Michelle was in her third year as a curate and had realized that the dancing was much more than a hobby. After the many years of not having danced, Michelle discovered that the physical activity of dancing was a key way of releasing any tension that had built up during the week. As it was a very different sort of dancing, she was able to experience it as a new form of exercise in which the music was central to her enjoyment. In addition, she was with a group of like-minded people. I shall return to this group aspect of the activity in Chapter 5.

Reflection

It is well known that exercise is good for our general health and well-being. Even during the strictest lockdown during the Covid pandemic, we were encouraged to take some form of exercise, especially outside. For many people it is a vital part of their weekly, if not daily, rhythm and a routine way of releasing stress and frustration. For others it is more a sense of duty – 'I ought to go for a walk'. Michelle did not enjoy running or walking, so that having discovered dance again was something to celebrate. In the past, dancing had been associated with her former husband and her grief about the end of the marriage. Now it was associated with her ministry training, her new friend and the joy of her ministry. She realized how much her body and soul had missed her dancing self and resolved to make her weekly class as important as her weekly meeting with the ministry team.

Active participation was highlighted as important by focus group members. Whenever we read a novel or watch a film or other performance, or go to an art exhibition, we have the opportunity to lose ourselves in a world that has been created for us by the author, film maker or artist. The experience may also nourish us aesthetically. It depends on our own interests whether or not we need that aesthetic nourishment. Some may draw a distinction between what I think of as survival switch-off and the deeper demands of a respected work of art. An example of the former might be to watch a soap opera and get temporary respite from work, whereas going to the cinema to see a new film would involve a deeper immersion into the art form and storyline.

The members of the first focus group indicated that they needed to set aside protected time for reading, drawing or going to the theatre. This could resource them both consciously and unconsciously. For example, in a fascinating study of the relationship between acting, spectating and the unconscious, Maria Turri offers a psychoanalytical perspective on unconscious processes of identification in the theatre, in which she suggests that the actor is receiving projections from the spectators. She draws on the psychoanalyst Wilfred Bion's theory of thinking, in which he distinguished between alpha-function, or thinking, and beta-elements, or 'thoughts without a thinker' (Symington and Symington, 1996, p. 102) and the role of projective identification of the mother or analyst in helping the development of the baby's or patient's mind. Turri suggests that the actor, through the character being played, provides an opportunity for the spectator. Projective identification is the process by which:

> the infant communicates his emotional state to his mother. Her ability to tolerate and process these feeling states, especially the frightening ones, enables the infant to take them back in a manageable form and also gradually to introject this capacity to process emotional experiences. (Symington and Symington, 1996, p. 154)

The analyst also offers a similar capacity to the patient, through interpreting the transference between them. Turri suggest that this trans-personal process also takes place in the theatre because

> the dynamic between sensibility and understanding in the art of the actor can ... be construed as an alpha-function: her

becoming the emotions of the character through her sensibility generates an act of understanding. Crucially, such understanding is directed at the character's emotions, not her own, according to a process which is known in theatre jargon as an 'interpretation'. (Turri, 2017, p. 100)

The actor is a conduit through which the emotional transaction takes place. Her or his work of interpretation is 'aimed at the impersonation of the character in front of an audience' (p. 100). A similar experience may be available during other performances that involve the inhabitation of characters, such as musicals or operas.

In a liturgical context, it could be said that this throws light on what can happen to clergy when presiding at the Eucharist. The president stands in for Christ as at the Last Supper and through the Holy Spirit blesses the bread and the wine, which are distributed to the congregation. This calls for an attitude of humility on the part of the priest, but this can lead to more being projected onto the person of the president. If the clergy person is vulnerable and lacking in confidence, there may be a danger of him or her introjecting the projections and really believing that he or she is very special and possibly indispensable. Hence the need for self-reflection, pastoral supervision and regular ministry reviews.

Theological resources

The members of the focus groups drew on a variety of theological resources when they reflected on their need to engage with the creative arts. These were wide-ranging, embracing the Creation and our role in becoming co-creators with God; the Christian mystics, including the use of icons; the regular experience of the Eucharist, whether as president or member of the congregation; and the Benedictine practice of prayer-work-study. The value of rhythm and habit were acknowledged, and I develop this important aspect of creative repair in Chapter 7.

In Chapter 9 some of these themes are taken up in a consideration of a possible theology of creative repair.

The context of ministry

One interesting outcome of the first focus group discussion was the importance of the context of ministry. Those who had worked as chaplains in sector ministries such as hospitals or prisons often had reviews and support built into their daily work. For those in parishes it was much less specific and left to the individual clergy person's initiative. In both parish and chaplaincy settings there was a recognition of the importance of a well-functioning ministry team. The style of respective leaders set the culture for the team, and it was hard to influence more authoritarian leaders.

The implications for theological and ministry training were not lost on my participants. They reported that attitudes were hard to shift. When tutors attempted to put more space into the week for their students, many students just filled the gaps with more activities. Nevertheless, there was agreement that good practice established during the time of ministerial formation could establish long-term habits of ongoing creative repair.

Conclusion

The members of the first focus group not only drew on their experience to affirm the importance of creative repair for their well-being but many of them also paid tribute to the value of responding to the questions, whether in the group or by email. It was as if the very exercise itself had been an experience of creative repair.

At first, I did not draw a distinction between the practice of creative repair as an individual and the benefit of being with others. It was the experience of the second focus group that highlighted the additional value of joining a group. Various participants evidenced the importance of being with others. The next chapter will focus on creative repair in a group, a practice that is particularly helpful as a prophylactic habit protecting those in a leadership role from the dangers of believing that they are indispensable.

5

Group Creative Repair

The poet John Donne famously wrote: 'No man is an island, entire of itself; every man is a piece of the continent, a part of the main' (1623, p. 131). As observed by members of the second focus group, it became clear that they identified the importance of others in their practice of creative repair. This might simply be being encouraged to resource themselves by a partner, family member or spiritual director. However, in some cases it meant the presence of others taking part in the same activity, such as circle or line dancing, singing in a choir or playing in a band. I had already noticed that my workshops with clergy and ordinands were often experienced as creative repair by the participants as a group in the here-and-now, but they were doubtful about their capacity to practise it when on their own in their parishes. As a group analyst I am profoundly convinced of the importance of our social selves. In this chapter, I shall briefly introduce the theory of group analysis founded by S. H. Foulkes before applying it to creative repair.

Group analysis

As human beings we are social through and through, and what can cause us stress and depression is external or internal isolation. Groups are essential. Group analysts have a particular view of groups and a training of several years equips them to facilitate or, as we would say, *conduct* group psychoanalytic psychotherapy. It is the treatment of choice for those who struggle with social isolation and other mental health issues, providing that they are psychologically minded and have sufficient Ego or inner strength to share the therapeutic space with others. Other settings in which groups are held may be less intense, yet can still be important experiences provided that they are conducted by those who are professionally trained or at the very least, in general settings, do no harm. Group analysts conduct groups in a wide range of health, forensic and educational settings. Reflective practice is commonplace within NHS mental health settings and counsellors in training are usually expected to have weekly sensitivity or experiential groups as an integral part of their training.

A group is 'more than people who happen to be doing the same thing at the same time in the same place' (Barnes, Ernst and Hyde, 1999, p. 2). 'A group is understood to be any number of people who interact with each other, are psychologically aware of each other and perceive themselves to be a group' (Stacey, 2003, p. 68). What makes a group is the relationship between group members who have a connection, a common purpose or task. There is a difference between the pianist who practises alone and the choir or orchestra who rehearse together, albeit with the help of a conductor.

The founder of group analysis, S. H. Foulkes, valued the term 'conductor' as an intentional reference to a musical conductor, who brings in each of the players or singers during the rehearsal or performance of a piece of music. This 'fluctuating location of authority between conductor and orchestra' (Behr and Hearst, 2005, p. 7) also connects with another influential feature of the evolution of Foulkesian group analysis: the gestalt idea of figure/ground in which 'figures of interest emerge from and recede into an undifferentiated ground, like the relationship between a wave and water' (Taylor, 2014, p. 42). One of the core principles of group analysis is that the conductor is also a group member so that although the group conductor does not introduce personal material, she or he moves in and out of an active leadership mode, and the more the group members are able to offer reflections or raise questions to one another, the less the conductor needs to say. Unlike those approaches to groups that can set the leader and group in a more binary position (Bion, 1961), the group analyst, arguably like any competent psychotherapist, works to become redundant, when the useful way of thinking modelled by the conductor has become internalized by group members.

Applying these ideas of a group conductor and figure/ground to creative repair in a group, I suggest that those clergy or faith leaders who are able to move between the leadership role of, say, conducting worship in the congregational group and the experience of being a member of a different group engaged in creative repair are likely to resource themselves both through the arts and by engagement with others. While I accept that some people find groups difficult, those with sufficient Ego strength to benefit from the presence of others as they practise creative repair may find themselves resourced in subtle ways that enrich them socially as well as individually. When, for example, out of their ministry role, they encounter others as co-creators in the context of the theatre or music group as they explore their creativity. This respite from the leadership role could be seen as a regular reminder that they do not need to be in charge all of the time.

In suggesting that there is value in letting go of a leadership role regularly and routinely, I am also drawing on my experience of conducting reflective staff groups within the NHS. Because I am employed to hold the boundaries of the group and facilitate the discussion, it becomes possible for the most junior member in the hierarchy to speak with candour to the most senior person present and vice versa. As the whole staff team are present and witness the encounters, reparation of previous hurts and misunderstandings can be experienced, even though there may be moments of discomfort. At first staff members are often unsure of the value of the reflective practice group, but experience teaches them that it is valuable and restorative. Although a music, art or theatre group may not be set up as a direct emotional resource for participants, it offers the opportunity for mutuality. Further, I would argue that, *mutatis mutandis*, the 'in charge' self is able to have respite from leadership and benefit from the need to fit in with others for the sake of a creative whole. The experience of Barry will help to make this clear.

Barry

Barry had been in ministry for seven years. Before being called to explore his vocation, he had been an English and drama teacher and believed that ordination involved leaving his previous life behind completely. During his curacy he had helped to run a youth group alongside learning his new role. His Training Incumbent and other colleagues were curious about his former life, but Barry was fully focused on his new ministry. When his colleagues suggested that he introduce drama to his youth group, he did not want to combine his past skills with his new context. His colleagues respected this but were puzzled.

After completing his curacy, Barry moved to a different diocese and was appointed as an associate priest in a rural benefice with a cluster of parishes. All was well until his senior colleague became ill and was diagnosed with Parkinson's disease. Gradually Barry took on more responsibility and eventually his colleague retired due to ill health. Barry was encouraged to apply for the senior position and was appointed in his sixth year of ministry. He continued to work hard and began to build up a ministry team of lay leaders and retired clergy. As the incumbent he had overall responsibility for the benefice, and the diocese told him that there was insufficient funding for a replacement associate priest. Over time he became increasingly stressed and was in danger of burning out.

At his Ministry Development Review (MDR), the reviewer asked Barry what he did to unwind and restore his energy. At first, he spoke of computer games and walks with his dog. The reviewer knew that Barry was single and asked about past ways of resourcing himself. After a while Barry remembered his old life as a teacher. He spoke wistfully of school productions and the local theatre group to which he had belonged, the smell of greasepaint, the camaraderie of the production team and the thrill of the performances. His reviewer invited him to look for a local theatre group, preferably beyond the parish boundaries and reclaim his old love of drama. Barry followed up the suggestion and found a theatre group in a nearby town. After a while, he regained his old energy, was able to relax with a new group of friends and let his hair down in a safe way. From then on, he put the rehearsal dates in his diary before setting dates for church meetings. In time he even began to write the occasional script, but resisted the invitation to produce a play himself. This was wise, as it would have put him in a leadership role while off duty.

Reflection

Barry had fallen into the common trap of splitting himself and his way of life into before and after his calling to ministry. Anxious to prove that he had benefited from his ministry training, and wanting to please his Training Incumbent, he had set aside his former life and failed to realize that he had unconsciously relied on his theatre activities to replenish the energy expended in teaching English to teenagers. The work culture in his school had been set by a rather driven, workaholic headmistress who expected all her staff to follow her example. As he routinely led drama workshops and organized school productions as part of his job, Barry had joined a local theatre group in order to keep his own acting skills fresh, almost as part of his paid work. On being ordained, he threw himself into ministry, in many ways a performing art, and did not seem to miss his old interest in theatre. This set a pattern for future ministry.

During his curacy, Barry was sufficiently resourced by his study days, computer games and walks with his dog. His Training Incumbent carried overall responsibility. During the early years of a new professional way of life, anxiety to prove oneself can mask the need for continuity with the person who used to be in a different way of life. Once he became an incumbent,

Barry's old ministry habits did not allow him to make proper provision for his increased emotional and psychological needs. He was heading for burnout. After he joined a theatre group it offered him regular respite from ministry in a different area, so that he was not known as the vicar. In addition, he had a break from being in a leadership role, able to be one of the actors and helping out where needed. He began to have scope for his own creativity and it was important that he resisted any invitation to be the producer with all the responsibility that would have entailed.

There are three key ideas to do with groups which indicate the value of being in a creative repair group such as a choir or theatre group. These are: first, the therapeutic value of being in a group; second, the implicit presence of the figure/ground dynamic of both gestalt and group analysis, which enables the potential isolation in leadership to be overcome; and third, the role of an attachment to the creative activity group, which facilitates a sense of belonging, itself an antidote to isolation. I will consider each of these ideas in more detail.

The therapeutic value of being in a group

The therapeutic value of being in a group was evidenced by my research. There are different uses of the word 'therapeutic'. Used in a technical sense, group-analytic psychotherapy is a therapeutic method that has been described as 'a rewarding and effective form of group psychotherapy' (Roberts, 1991, p. 3). A therapeutic method is a recognized professional way of treating those who seek help either for their psychological and emotional distress or for personal development needs. Used more broadly, experiences that enhance psychological and emotional health can be described as therapeutic.

Applied to other settings, people learn about themselves in a group. Although the participants are not engaged in therapy as such, their respective creativity groups are useful in the sense that they have the opportunity to learn about themselves through reflecting on their experience of being part of their groups. Given the importance of self-knowledge in the criteria of selection of Church of England clergy, this is one setting in which that capacity can be developed. It also allows them a regular, ordinary way of sustaining their psychological health and well-being.

Group analysts work in various settings, applying the principles and practice of group analysis to the particular setting involved. There are open groups, which have a fluid membership and in some cases are even drop-in groups, and closed groups, in which new members are introduced when others leave. New members are brought in mindfully and in discussion with existing group members. Beyond their use in technically therapeutic settings, both in the private and public sector, groups are also widely used in many organizational settings. There are theories about the stages of development of a group. One popular way of describing these stages in the life of groups is as 'forming, storming, norming and performing' (Tuckman, 1965, p. 396). In other words, a group may come together initially to form itself as a group; then after apparent initial conformity, differences may emerge that lead to conflict; if this is well managed, the group moves to a phase of establishing norms or ways of managing difference; finally, the group functions well in the task for which it has been established. However, those involved in groups rarely consider the dynamics at work, which may explain why there are various formal or ad hoc groups that are 'liked by their members or regarded as a waste of time' (Handy, 1993, p. 150).

During the period of mourning after the death of Queen Elizabeth II on 8 September 2022, there were several days when the Queen's body lay in state in Westminster Hall. Members of the general public queued for many hours in order to walk past the catafalque and 'pay their respects' as many of them described it. The media interviewed people as they queued and there were references to groups of people who found themselves near to each other in the queue. They formed ad hoc groups, some saying that they had made new friends, or even that they had a new 'family'. Far from seeing them as a waste of time, these groups had given meaning to those queuing, rather as fellow pilgrims value the experience of meeting others when journeying to a holy place.

In order for creative repair groups to be beneficial, leadership needs to be thoughtful and clear: Music therapist Gary Ansdell suggests that 'the benefits of any group experience rely on ongoing cultivation and careful management' (2015, p. 200). This comment could also apply to other groups, such as those to which my research participants belonged. Their positive experience of their creative activity groups indicated that their shared task was clear, the leadership was well enough conducted and the life cycle of their particular creative activity group had reached the effective or performative stage. Considering that creative repair groups such as theatre groups, choirs, or other musical groups, for example, bands or orchestras, are often rehearsing for an actual performance in one of the creative arts, there is a double sense in which the performing stage of a group's life cycle is facilitated by a shared goal. The combination of the group and creativity progressing towards a shared performance can be particularly beneficial.

Figure/ground and a flexible mindset

Incumbents such as Barry are particularly vulnerable to isolation due to their exposure as leaders, because the overall responsibility rests with them even if they have others in their ministry teams (Ison, 2005, pp. ix–x). A psychodynamic understanding of the dynamic between leaders and followers highlights the need for leaders not to be invested in their role for personal affirmation, or it can lead to grandiosity (Watts, Nye and Savage, 2002, p. 69). The complexity and potential hiddenness of this process are shown by the fact that even the therapist who becomes ordained (who understands this in theory) is not always aware of what is going on in a ministry setting, as David Runcorn has powerfully recorded. Despite all his professional experience of 'transference' and group dynamics, he was quite unprepared for the sheer weight and power of projected hopes and expectations that he experienced in his new role in the community (2005, p. 25).

Those individual incumbents who took part in my research indicated their awareness of the weight of their role and the consequent need for respite from the pressures of leadership. The criteria for selection imply the need for flexibility of mind (Church of England, 2014, p. 15). Although the context for this is the capacity to be receptive to different intellectual perspectives, it could usefully be applied to the need to oscillate between leadership and membership roles in the practice of ministry. If so, then there would perhaps need to be a critical conversation between those theologies of ministry that emphasize the permanent nature of priesthood and charismatically anointed leadership, thus exacerbating the danger of grandiosity and the need for genuine flexibility in ministry practice.

A relevant model for a flexible mindset is to be found in the gestalt idea of figure/ground. The idea of figure/ground that is common both to group analysis and gestalt therapy helps to explain the need of the incumbents to be members of their creative activity groups. As noted earlier there has been a comparison between figure and ground and wave and water (Taylor, 2014, p. 42). Applied to my individual participants and other leaders, by belonging to their creative activity groups they had respite from being the 'figure' as ministry leaders by being members or part of the 'ground' of their group, in which someone else was leading.

Foulkes favoured the word 'conductor' for the group therapist or facilitator, as an orchestral metaphor for his or her role in helping each of the group members to find their voice in the group, rather as a musical conductor brings in each of the instruments when they are playing a piece of music together. In a Foulkesian group-analytic group, whether it is an actual therapy group or an applied group conducted on group-analytic principles, the focus moves fluidly between group members, including the conductor. She or he sometimes responds to the 'figure' of the particular person speaking or the 'ground' of what is happening in the group-as-a-whole. This involves a flexibility of mind and the capacity to move between the roles of group member and conductor, rather as the location of authority moves between conductor and players (Behr and Hearst, 2005, p. 7). As part of continuing professional development, group analysts are encouraged to attend study days that include a group experience in which a colleague is in the role of conductor. This reinforces their experience of being in a membership role, so that they model the capacity to move between being the figure and being part of the ground. In other words, group analysts are obliged through such experiences to have a flexible experience, a check and balance against self-idealization or grandiosity.

Incumbents and other faith leaders are routinely in a leadership role. 'To be the spiritual leader is to be a powerfully symbolic figure in the community' (Runcorn, 2005, p. 25). It is easy for them to become dependent on the affirmation that comes from such a role and therefore vulnerable to an unrealistic and unhealthy view of themselves. They can also become very isolated in their leadership role. If they are able to move in and out of leadership/membership roles they are less dependent on being the one in charge, in receipt of all the negative or idealized projections sustained by leaders (Rose, 2013, p. 30), and more likely to sustain their ministry. Although the individual participants in my research were not, to my knowledge, aware of the principles of group analysis or gestalt therapy, their membership of their respective creativity groups indicated and helped them to develop an implicit flexibility of mind. The fact that they all demonstrated their capacity to be flexible between roles and associated their time off with membership rather than leadership indicates that they were potentially protected from some of the danger of self-importance caused by the dual roles of clergy. Whereas other professional people such as doctors or solicitors will usually only meet people in their surgeries or offices, clergy and other faith leaders meet people informally in pastoral or social settings as well as in their worship leader role and this can lead to a confusion between the role and the person. The human being who is in the role may come to believe that she or he is indispensable to others, at worst succumbing to a saviour complex. The habit of moving between figure and ground in a creative repair group can help to prevent this hazard of the role.

It is not necessary to understand the theory of group analysis in order to benefit from the practice of being in a group. However, it would be helpful if clergy were to have more experience of groups during their training. For example, many counsellors and psychotherapists will have experience of being in a sensitivity group during their clinical training, but few will be familiar with the group-analytic theory lying behind their experience. The experience of being a member of a group of fellow trainees helps their growing self-knowledge and complements the individual experience of therapy usually required by such training. As they are also learning the role of counsellor, the group offers them an opportunity to receive from other group members as well as the group conductor while they are getting used to the responsibility of the role of therapist. They regularly move between roles of figure and ground.

In a parallel way, a key benefit of their experience of their creative repair groups for my individual research participants was the opportunity to be in a membership rather than a leadership role. This resourced their ministry as well as resourcing them personally. For example, a singer could be part of the ground, when singing confidently in a choir, and this supports their role as the figure when singing the leading role in the liturgy. An orchestral player could move flexibly between being part of the ground of the brass and woodwind sections and an occasional role as a soloist or figure in the orchestra. As one person put it: 'You could have a little section within the orchestral part where the trumpet's supposed to play something that's marked *piano*, but it could actually be a solo and could be important that it comes out and is heard,' whereas at other times 'you have to just keep part of the general sound'.

The experience of being sometimes the figure and sometimes

the ground in their respective creative activity groups helped those in leadership roles to have respite from the projections and demands of leadership and meant that they implicitly practised the flexibility of figure/ground. Given the danger of self-idealization for those who are leaders in ministry settings, this regular group experience acts as a prophylactic against an occupational hazard. In addition, it protects them from the possibility of burnout from over-responsibility and the refusal or inability to get into a different mode. Their regular experience of being fed rather than feeding others consolidates a sense of reciprocity in ministry, itself a protection against grandiosity. An additional factor was the participants' attachment to their respective groups, an idea to which I now turn.

Attachment to a group

Members of a creative repair group become attached to their groups. This is important both in terms of the importance of belonging to a group outside the ministry setting and because attachment to a particular creative activity group is a key part of creative repair in a group. Two theoretical traditions contribute to an understanding of this: first, attachment theory and, second, an understanding of a hierarchy of needs.

The psychologist John Bowlby, who studied the relationships between young infants and their parents, suggested that from childhood we all need a secure base from which to develop:

> In a given child the complex of behavioural systems mediating attachment comes into being because in the ordinary family environment in which the vast majority of children are raised these systems grow and develop in a comparatively stable way. (1969, p. 265)

Since Bowlby developed his thinking, attachment theory has grown and developed and become a therapeutic modality in its own right (Holmes, 2001). While there has been some interest in attachment theory among some group analysts, it has not been part of core group-analytic theory. It is theory-in-progress because there are some group analysts, notably Glenn (1987), Marrone (1994, 2014) and Esquerro (2017), who have applied attachment theory to the practice of group analysis. Attachment to a group can be important for survival, 'particularly at times when people are pressed into a collaborative and egalitarian struggle against a common enemy' (Esquerro, 2017, p. 93). When clergy are going through difficult times, either in their parish or more widely, feeling that they are working against a tide of secularism, their attachment to their creative activity groups can support their survival and sense of integrity.

Sometimes peer-group attachments established at an early age can be fundamental to children's survival in the absence of individual attachments (Esquerro, 2017, p. 108). Secondary attachments to siblings, peers and groups can contribute substantially to a child's development and can mitigate problems with primary attachment figures. Applied to the adult, an attachment to a peer group in training can offer an alternative safe base from which to explore new ways of relating to others while learning a new discipline. The group can dilute the sense of isolation that individuals can feel when developing in new directions. As an example, during a Foundation Course in Group Analysis, a colleague observed that when the visiting seminar leader asked the students to form two groups according to their professional interests, consciously or unconsciously they formed exactly the same groups that met later for their experiential group. This was only recognized in the staff feedback session afterwards. While it could have been a genuine coinciding with their professional interests, it was more likely to have been a need to stay in a safe zone while learning new ideas. The experience of Sandra serves to illustrate the importance of attachment to a creative repair group.

Sandra

Sandra had been a pastoral counsellor attached to a northern diocese for about ten years. She often had referrals of clergy or their spouses who had found themselves in difficult circumstances. Having grown up in a Christian family, she was in tune with many of the ethical dilemmas that emerged in the work. After a particularly complex case involving domestic abuse, she began to lose her capacity to absorb the emotional content of the work, especially because it had touched a raw nerve in her own past. In her regular supervision session, she confided in her supervisor that she feared that she was in danger of compassion fatigue. Her supervisor had already noticed a subtle change and explored with Sandra what she did to resource herself when not working. It emerged that Sandra had been part of a writing group but, having moved house too far away to return to it, she had stopped producing the short stories and poems she used to write when prompted by the meetings of the group. She had been very attached to the group and hadn't got round to finding another one, unable to face starting again with new people. Her supervisor encouraged her to contact her old group and ask if anyone could introduce her to a new group nearer to her new home. Not only was she missing the release and renewal which her writing gave her, but she also missed the companionship of other writers and a regular group that was entirely different from her professional colleagues. Sandra followed this up and it turned out that one of the members of her old group had a sister near to her new home who also belonged to a writing group. Even before meeting the new group for the first time, Sandra began writing again, knowing that she had a context in which to share her work. She negotiated a month's unpaid leave from her diocese, after which she returned to work with her old enthusiasm and capacity to draw emotional boundaries between her clients and herself.

Reflection

Sandra's experience demonstrated how difficult it can be to maintain appropriate empathic detachment when dealing with difficult situations, especially when there were echoes of incidents in her own past. Although she had been in counselling herself as part of her training, and was therefore aware of her raw spots, she sensed in time that her capacity to manage the emotional weight of the work was vulnerable. As part of her professional role she routinely had supervision, so that she already had a safe place in which she could consider her situation. Her supervisor noticed that Sandra was not her usual self. Aware that there had been a recent house move, she explored the impact of the dislocation and helped Sandra to identify her loss of the writing group. The positive aspects of the move had masked the loss of this group. Sandra's attachment to her former group was understandable, not only because she missed the other group members, but also because it held the history of many of her stories and poems. Starting again with new people seemed too difficult. However, encouraged by her supervisor and needing to regain her confidence in her professional self, Sandra recognized the role of a writing group in routinely resourcing her. The structure of the supervision sessions, her own self-awareness and her commitment to the work gave her the courage to negotiate a professional break, recover from the move and find the new group. What she had unconsciously thought was a desirable but non-essential aspect of her life had been shown to be a central part of her personal support structure. Introduced to the new group by the sister of her former writing friend, she soon settled in and reclaimed her creativity. By taking action in time, she avoided the danger of burnout, with its consequent professional and personal crisis. It also enabled her to model implicit good practice to her clergy clients, although they would not know what had been happening to her in her personal life.

Clergy in role find that 'personal friendship and intimacy are rarely achieved' (Peyton and Gatrell, 2013, p. 129), partly due to the need to maintain professional boundaries within their parish. Curates have been advised: 'Everyone has friends who inspire, friends to have a good time with, and friends who drain. When time to socialize is at a premium, spend that time with people you really want to be with' (Pedrick and Clutterbuck, 2005, p. 126).

The evidence of my research indicated the importance of shared interests with others in their creative activity groups. Clergy may become very attached to their parishes, which can make it difficult when they have to leave them. It is important that they have groups outside their ministry settings to which they can attach reliably over time. This can be very important when clergy retire and have to let go of their parish. One person who had managed to keep her membership of a choir active during the last years of ministry regarded it as a key part of the future after retirement. No longer would there be a clash between choir rehearsals and performances and the needs of ministry. She would be free from all past obligations, and this was something to look forward to. Her attachment to her choir both protected her from burnout and acted as an agent of continuity after ministry.

The need to be with others is partly explained by another theoretical tradition, initiated by A. H. Maslow, who outlined his recognition of a hierarchy of needs in the 1950s. He believed that once the basic physiological needs of food, water and shelter and the physical need of safety have been met, 'there will emerge the love and affection and belongingness needs' (1954, p. 89). Not only will the person feel the absence of close relatives and friends, but 'will hunger for affectionate relations with people in general, namely, for a place in his [sic] group and he will strive with great intensity to achieve this goal' (p. 89). As one colleague has put it:

> Groups, both formal and informal, meet human needs for affiliation and self-esteem. They provide individuals with a sense of security, they reduce anxiety and the sense of powerlessness and they provide opportunities for individuals

to test reality through discussion with others. (Stacey, 2003, p. 69)

The need for clergy to belong to a group outside the parish in which they serve is highlighted by their potential isolation. 'The networks clergy belong to will vary, but the principle of taking time for friendships, fellowship and support is important' (Lawson, 2005, p. 45), especially as many incumbents work alone.

Conclusion

All those who work in settings in which the demands of the role can leave them feeling isolated can benefit from a creative repair group. These groups can be therapeutic in the broad sense that they enhance members' psychological and emotional health. The implicit way in which members can experience flexibility through alternating between leadership and membership of their creative activity groups is a living out of the figure/ground concept used in both group analysis and gestalt thinking in an applied way as a prophylactic to the dangers of grandiosity. Members' attachment to their groups affirms the value of bringing together groups and attachment theory, a growing idea within the practice of group analysis. Taken together with Maslow's hierarchy of needs, and the need to belong, the creative repair group offers an essential benefit to all its members. Not only is there the contribution to well-being which comes from creative repair in itself, but the opportunity to sing or act or play and participate in a non-leadership way also restores the energy expended in demanding professional or voluntary roles involving helping or pastoral activity.

6

The Creative Repair of Things

'Things play you up!' This response to something falling off a table or somehow disappearing into a pile of papers is clearly a projection. Inanimate objects do not move of their own accord. The phrase indicates our connection to actual objects, as distinct from our relationship to the person who is the object of our affections. Yet things or objects can carry enormous personal meaning or cultural significance. In his first foray into detective fiction, Richard Coles has given an example of the personal meaning of an object:

> It was only a biscuit tin, but it was as precious to him as a reliquary, even if its contents were plain chocolate digestives rather than the withered finger of a discalced Carmelite. It was the biscuit tin of his childhood, salvaged from his parents' bungalow after his father's death, and brought to the rectory. It had been a wedding present, rather a modest one he thought, but had served for more than half a century, and for that reason contained more than biscuits. It contained promise, reward, satisfaction: and memory too, as sure a key to that lock as Proust's madeleine. (2022, p. 14)

Any museum is full of objects that represent our cultural or historical past as human beings. Occupations such as those of archaeologists or archivists, restorers or valuers rely on our interest in the importance of things as a part of our heritage. In this chapter I shall consider the way in which we relate to things both personally and culturally. The respective themes are the place of things in history as well as in our families. I shall draw on Neil MacGregor's *History of the World in 100 Objects* (2010), and the extraordinary success of the BBC programme *The Repair Shop*, as well as the Japanese art of *kintsugi*. I shall include one or two personal stories, referring to an original edition of the King James Bible, a priest's wartime Communion set, and the broken pottery piece known as Daisy the Cow. Finally, I shall consider the importance of toys or other transitional objects and comment on the role of Paddington Bear during the mourning period after the death of Queen Elizabeth II. Readers can perhaps reflect on their own experience of things or objects.

The History of the World in 100 Objects

Neil MacGregor's aim both in his BBC Radio Four series and subsequent book was not simply to describe the objects but to show their significance. Telling the stories of the objects has often led to a re-examination of certain aspects of historical assumptions. Chosen by colleagues from the British Museum and the BBC, they ranged in date from the beginning of human history around two million years ago to the present day. Intended to represent as many countries in the world as possible and from a range of contexts, they included objects of everyday life as well as those belonging to the rich and powerful. One of the attractive aspects of the series was that the history which emerged through the objects was not familiar to most people. It complemented that discovered through the examination of written texts. Some cultures such as the Moche culture of Peru survive solely through the archaeological record (MacGregor, 2010, p. xvii). As a consequence, the Moche are central to a rethinking of the American past (p. 307). I have chosen three of the 100 objects, representing different periods and civilizations.

Chinese Bronze Bell – Bronze bell, found in Shanxi province, China. 500–400 BC[1]

Bells play an important part in Chinese history and go back thousands of years. As MacGregor records, at the time when this bell was first played there was a period of instability and a 'lively intellectual debate about what an ideal society ought to be, and by far the most famous and influential contributor to these debates was Confucius who placed a very high value on peace and harmony' (p. 191). He cites Confucius as saying: 'Music produces a kind of pleasure which human nature cannot do without' (p. 191). This takes the idea of creative repair into a higher level of significance, because music was seen as 'a metaphor of a harmonious society, and its performance could actually help bring that better society about' (p. 191). Some would say that music is a truly international language; Confucius believed in the importance of music in education and that it helped to build a harmonious society. This bell would not have been played alone but would have once been part of either nine or 14 bells. Each would have been a different size and would have produced two different tones, depending on where it was struck (p. 193). When perfectly tuned alongside other bells, the bell would have contributed to the sense of diversity and harmony that is so much a part of Confucius' philosophy. A set of ancient bells was played both at the 1997 ceremony marking Britain's handover of Hong Kong to the People's Republic of China and at the 2008 Olympic Games in Beijing.

Moche Warrior Pot – Clay pot, from Peru. AD 100–700

This three-dimensional clay figure with its clothes and weapons, the way it was made and the site of its burial have contributed to the reconstruction of a lost civilization. Whereas the Aztecs and the Incas are well-established in our cultural history, the Moche people are virtually unknown, yet they built a society 'that incorporated probably the first real state structure in the whole of South America' (p. 307). Situated in the narrow strip of land between the Andes Mountains and the Pacific Ocean, the civilization lasted for more than 800 years, roughly between 200 BC to around AD 650. As the Moche left no writing it is accessible to us only through archaeology. This pot can be seen in the British Museum with other South American pots, which comprise 'a pottery representation of the Moche universe' (p. 309). They were master potters, their expertise affirmed by Grayson Perry: 'You imagine the person who's made it has made hundreds of these things, and they're incredibly confident when they're making it' (as cited by MacGregor, 2010, p. 309).

The largest Moche settlement, found near the modern Peruvian city of Trujillo, was 'the first real city in South America, with streets, canals, plazas and industrial areas that any contemporary Roman town would have been proud of' (p. 310), as MacGregor puts it with characteristic enthusiasm. The various clay pots indicate the link between war and religion because they seem to have been made for burials and sacrifice. It is speculated that climate change in the form of several decades of intense rain followed by drought contributed to the decline of the Moche state and civilization in the seventh century.

Early Victorian Tea Set – Stoneware and silver tea set, from Staffordshire, England. AD 1840–1845

By contrast, the early Victorian tea set, MacGregor's 92nd object, does not tell us about the origin of a civilization but indicates the way in which world trade and imperial history have affected the habits of millions of people living in the British Isles. The tea set is 'made up of three pieces of red-brown stoneware: a smallish teapot about 14 centimetres (6 inches) high with a short straight spout, a sugar bowl and a milk jug' (MacGregor, 2010, p. 601). The different items of the tea set each represent aspects of trading and farming history, some of it linked to British colonial history. The tea was imported from India or China, often sweetened by sugar from the Caribbean.

> Behind the modern British cup of tea lie the high politics of Victorian Britain, the stories of nineteenth-century empire, of mass production and of mass consumption, the taming of an industrial working class, the reshaping of the agriculture of continents, the movement of millions of people, and a world-wide shipping industry (p. 601).

Made at Wedgwood's Etruria factory in Stoke-on-Trent, the silver-decorated tea set was an elaborate version of a range aimed at quite modest households. Tea had become popular among the upper classes before 1700. In time, tea replaced alcohol as a safer form of daily fluid than water, which was often contaminated. Since then, it has become a form of social glue, a resource in times of distress and at times a source of amusement to others, as expressed in the humorous 'More tea, Vicar?' Many a newly ordained clergyperson has learned the importance of receiving such basic hospitality when making pastoral visits. While coffee has more recently replaced tea as the standard beverage for many British people, tea remains the drink which symbolizes a way of life hard-wired in the psyche of those who grew up in the second half of the twentieth century. More than a drink, it represents kindness at a time of shock and a transitional state in which many people can process difficult experiences.

The Repair Shop

For some years there has been a regular programme shown on BBC television called *The Repair Shop*. People bring in various objects that have been in their families or communities, often for many generations, but have been damaged in some way. The founder, Jay Blades, has drawn together craftspeople who are very experienced and bring about remarkable restorations without losing the patina or other evidence of the object's history. As Blades has put it: 'Everyone has a story to tell. For those who can link their family history to a symbolic object, we at the Repair Shop can play a role in its retelling. We feel privileged at becoming a small part of that history' (Farrington, 2020, p. viii). Among the many examples are a Jamaican pump organ, a foundling's teddy and a Bletchley Park bicycle.[2]

A Jamaican pump organ

When Vera McKenzie left Kingston, Jamaica, in response to the call for workers to rebuild Britain after the Second World War, among her few possessions was a pump organ or harmonium. It was a gift from her music teacher and for several years would be at the heart of her family and religious life. Such portable pump organs were designed for long-haul travel and were used by Christian missionaries across the world. Having joined her husband Mack who had preceded her to Britain, and despite experiencing racism, they kept things together partly helped by the music Vera played on the pump organ. They brought up two daughters and Vera also looked after other children near them while their parents were at work. As the pump organ deteriorated, Mack attempted to repair it, but the repair proved disastrous and the organ was unplayable. After Vera and Mack died, the organ went to their daughter Carmen and her husband as a memento of Vera until it came to the Repair Shop.

Expert David Burville took the organ apart and discovered damage to some of the keys and valves, probably caused years ago by a spilt drink. The main problem was that creases in the bellows cloth had split, through age and use. By applying leather to worn areas, and coating everything in a rubber solution to disguise the patches, David made the bellows airtight again. After replacing the webbing that allowed the foot pedals to flex and cleaning all the reeds, the instrument could be played again. The case was re-polished before the organ was returned to the sisters Carmen and Angela. It is now kept in Angela's house and she plays it in memory of her parents. Angela commented, 'Mum was a woman of few words, although when she talked, everyone listened. As a young woman she would always choose to play rather than speak. Now it feels like she is being heard again in our family' (Farrington, 2020, p. 16). Not only was this repair of the organ important as an object carrying much family history, it was also a trans-generational example of the role of music in repairing the pain of grief for Vera when she left her Jamaican home and easing the wounds of racism which she and Mack experienced when they first came to England.

A foundling's teddy

Amanda and Julie, known as the 'teddy bear ladies', are mistresses of projection. Whatever the backstory of the dolls and soft toys brought in for repair, they immediately identify with the owners' memories of these precious survivors of often difficult experiences. One example is the teddy bear brought in by Lesley. As a baby, Lesley was left on the doorstep of Mary and John, a childless couple, just after the Second World War. In time they were able to foster, then adopt her and she grew up knowing herself to be loved unconditionally. One of the first gifts that Mary bought her was a teddy bear, 'which became Lesley's lifelong confidante, taking pride of place on her bed' (Farrington, 2020, p. 69).

The psychoanalyst Donald Winnicott identified the function of significant cuddly and other toys or blankets as transitional objects.[3] As a baby develops and becomes aware of the comings and goings of his or her mother or other special person, the toy becomes a link to that person and gives the baby some security through this associated attachment. The presence of the transitional object is often essential for times such as going to sleep or travelling. Such toys may be discarded later, but for some children the attachment remains, as was the case with Lesley and Ted. Her attempt to clean Ted had been almost catastrophic, as the bear had caught fire while being left to dry in front of an electric bar fire. The scorched bear was bundled into a bag and left for some 50 years. As 'he' was a symbol of all the love that she had been given since being left on her parents' doorstep, Lesley brought Ted to the Repair Shop for restoration. Julie and Amanda identified Ted as a Chiltern bear, made in Chesham, Buckinghamshire, in the 1940s. They restored the bear as much as possible, using appropriate materials to repair the scorched areas and replacing the stuffing. Their colleague Steve repaired the original growler so that Lesley was delighted with the end result, affirming: 'Today he is wonderful. You would never know that I had toasted him. My parents always knew Ted was my comfort blanket. They would be pleased to know that he can come out again where everyone can see what a wonderful little bear he is' (Farrington, 2020, p. 76). There was something redemptive about the bear being restored that released Lesley from the guilt she had felt about having 'toasted' the bear in the past.

A Bletchley Park bicycle

This bicycle, brought into the Repair Shop by its former owner's son Huw, held more than family memories. It was given to Rachel Lawrence as an 18-year-old undergraduate in 1937, when she was studying at St Hilda's College, Oxford. It is not known how she was recruited to Bletchley Park, the Buckinghamshire stately home that had been turned into a secret cipher centre, but she worked there from 1941 as a cryptanalyst, specializing in the analysis and decryption of enemy ciphers. There she rode the bicycle to get around the estate. Working in Hut 6, the task for her and her colleagues across all the huts was to decipher endless coded messages generated by the German Enigma machine. Building on the work of Poland's Cipher Bureau carried out just before the outbreak of war, Alan Turing had a key role in breaking the German Enigma codes. He designed the Bombe machines, able to detect the Enigma 'keys' automatically. He focused on the German naval codes and was able to read the code in real time, just as considerable merchant shipping was being sunk in the Atlantic. As a result of this intelligence, British shipping was able to avoid the U-boats and the supply line was protected. Information gathered in Hut 6 was pivotal to the war in North Africa, in addition to picking up communications by the Italian armed forces and by the Japanese after Pearl Harbour.

An unintended benefit of her work in Hut 6 was Rachel's meeting Michael Banister and they married in the spring of 1944. Their son Huw knows little of their romance, as they had both signed the Official Secrets Act and later accepted a self-imposed amnesia of their wartime experience. Tribute was paid to the work at Bletchley Park by General Dwight D. Eisenhower, Supreme Allied Commander, who wrote: 'The intelligence which has emanated from you before and during the campaign has been of priceless value to me. It has amplified my task as a commander enormously. It has saved thousands of British and American lives' (cited in Farrington, 2020, p. 86).

After the war, the couple had four boys and Rachel used the bicycle to carry them around on shopping trips. When it was brought to the Repair Shop, the paintwork was fairly sound and the wheels were true, despite many years of being stored in a shed. It needed a new saddle, and bicycle expert Tim Gunn found a replacement sprocket drawn from vintage stock. Replacements were the minimum needed to make the bike roadworthy. One interesting discovery was a few specks of white paint, indicating a white patch painted on the rear mudguard, enough to alert other road users at a time when lights on bicycles were illegal during after-dark blackouts.

For Tim, as he test-rode the restored bicycle, it represented a secret past in Bletchley Park. For Huw it also brought back memories of being perched on it as a boy. Thereafter, he made a point of riding it once a week, 'reflecting on this vintage workhorse, with its years of sterling service freely given to education and the nation, to children and to chores' (p. 89).

The Japanese art of *kintsugi*

Kintsugi, which translates as 'golden joinery', is the ancient Japanese art of repairing what has been broken. Whereas ceramic repair, as practised by the brilliant Kirsten Ramsey of the Repair Shop, aims to restore the broken piece invisibly, the masters of *kintsugi* repair the piece with gold, so that the reconstruction is very visible. The reason for this is that for them a repaired piece symbolizes fragility, strength and beauty. According to Tomas Navarro, the first known *kintsugi* master, in the sixteenth century, was Chojiro, and his first pupil was Sokei (Navarro, 2018, p. xiv). In his book, *Kintsugi*, Navarro draws a comparison between ceramics and people. They share the qualities of strength, fragility and beauty. An experienced psychotherapist, Navarro offers readers a way of managing life in a *kintsugi*-influenced way. Imperfections can be embraced, rather than blamed, and our emotional scars can be accepted and integrated into the rest of our lives.

Kintsugi as a metaphor has also been adopted by Justine Allain-Chapman as part of a Lent book encouraging readers to move from adversity to maturity. She writes:

> The philosophy behind this art of broken pieces is that nothing is truly broken. Using gold is an extravagance, you could argue, because it is cheaper to replace a piece of broken pottery than to mend it. The break, however, is an important part of the object's history and becomes more precious than it was before. (2018, p. 90)

The principle can be applied to our own experience of damage or suffering. As Allain-Chapman puts it: 'Our wounds make us who we are, but healed, we are used again' (p. 91).

One of the aims of psychotherapy is to make sense of our experience, rather than to package it up and discard it. Of course, it is not suitable for everyone, but the so-called talking cure in which a person shares experience with a trained and trustworthy other in complete confidence can make a huge difference. By looking experience in the eye, acknowledging our own part in what has happened and bearing any shame that arises from the memories, it is possible to see experience as an opportunity for learning and a resource for the times when we listen to others.

The King James Bible

One day an elderly lady gave her local vicar, my father, an old Bible. It had been in her family, but now there was no one left to pass it on to. After my father's death, my mother gave it to me, as she thought I would find out what to do with it. For a long time it sat with other books, until I met someone with a personal link with the Bodleian Library in Oxford. After examining it carefully, he said that it was a first edition. I learned that there is a particular verse in the book of Ruth with a printing error. If the error is uncorrected, then it is a first edition. His suggestion was that I donate it to an institution which could have the considerable damage repaired. As they already had one in the Bodleian, an Oxford College might be one option. As I already had a strong link with Magdalen College – I had met my former husband when he was an undergraduate there, and later I had taught at Magdalen College School – I approached the then Dean of Divinity, who consulted the College Librarian. As it was possible for the College to restore it, I donated it to the College in memory of my father. It now resides alongside other rare books in the Old Library of Magdalen College.

This opportunity for the Bible's restoration also worked creatively for my former husband who was dying of pancreatic cancer. It meant a lot to him that I had become a benefactor to his old College and it was also helpful in enabling me to let go of some of the difficulties in our marriage and allowed me to focus on the sadness of losing an old friend who was the father of my children. Some further emotional repair took place some years later, when both my children, their spouses and their children met in the Old Library at Magdalen and saw the Bible in its appropriate setting, preserved for the future.

The Second World War communion set

One of the items brought to the Repair Shop was a Second World War Communion set that had been used by an RAF Chaplain to give Communion to servicemen when abroad, notably those coming back from prison camps in the Far East. The team were very struck by the history of this item and the stories that it represented. Since the war it has been used as a home Communion set, taken round to sick parishioners by the priest to whom the set had been given. He commented, 'They're not on the front line, but it still means as much to them.'

During the Second World War, my father, then in a post-curacy position as what was then called Succentor of Leicester Cathedral, signed up as a Chaplain in the Royal Air Force and spent the years from 1942 to 1945 in the Far East, serving in India and Burma. At my ordination, my widowed mother gave me my father's Communion set, identical to the one brought to the Repair Shop and in better condition. I have read some of his letters and although they were censored, they give a flavour of his travels, including long train journeys in India and experiences of life with the Forces. After his return he was called to parish life and used the Communion set for visiting the sick and dying.

Like many who returned after the end of the war, especially those who returned home later than VE day, it was a huge transition. As recorded in Melvyn Bragg's novel *The Soldier's Return* (1999), for which the author drew on his own experience, it was a difficult re-entry into the world they had left, changed as they had been by their experiences. Meanwhile any children left behind had grown and developed without their father present. My older sister was three years old when our father left and seven when he returned. Although he and my mother exchanged regular letters, which kept alive their own relationship, the lack of regular contact made it hard to sustain a lively sense of a child's development. One of the family narratives is that they didn't recognize each other on his return and that their relationship took time to recover. As I was born soon after his return, the Communion set is a link both to his wartime experience and his ministry during my formative years. Whenever I use it, I am aware of this trans-generational connection and wonder who else has received Holy Communion with this special set.

Daisy the Cow – a repaired object

Sometimes the most ordinary things can begin to tell a story. During the first year of the Covid pandemic in 2020, I got to know more of the local shopkeepers, as I took my daily walk round the village. One of them was the butcher and I noticed that he had several pottery cows on a shelf above the shop fridge. One was broken, so I offered to mend it with some porcelain cement. I was told that her name was Daisy. I stuck the pieces together. Not quite *kintsugi*, but I tied a ribbon with a little bell around its neck. The butcher was delighted and Daisy was reunited with her companions on the shelf. Some months later, he announced that he was leaving in order to have more time with his family. Unsure about Daisy's future, I offered to give her a home if that would help. After a day or two's reflection, he accepted my offer and knew that I would look after her. I placed her on a hall table from my parents' house next to a rabbit ornament. One morning before the butcher was leaving, I took a photo of Daisy in her new abode. I showed the butcher my photo and he commented that he knew she would be well looked after and was glad that she had Peter Rabbit to keep her company. All this was said tongue in cheek, but there was a serious sense of continuity of care behind the humour. Without the context of the butcher and the pandemic, it would just be a cow ornament. The new butcher was introduced to me and I was identified as the mender of Daisy. Small things can have meaning beyond their material identity.

The role of toys, Paddington Bear and the death of Her Majesty Queen Elizabeth II

As indicated in the description of a foundling's teddy, cuddly toys are known in the discipline of psychoanalysis as transitional objects. This dates to the work of Donald Winnicott, who famously coined the expression of the 'good-enough mother'[4] (1965/1990, p. 145). A good-enough mother gives the infant what he or she needs while allowing some frustration so that the child learns to try new things and make developmental progress. Part of this is the need to separate from the mother at times, including bedtime. 'Sooner or later in an infant's development there comes a tendency on the part of the infant to weave other-than-me objects into the personal pattern' (Winnicott, 1971, p. 3). For some this takes the form of sucking a thumb or fingers and for many infants, attachment to a cloth or special toy or teddy becomes the way of coping with the separation. The toy acts as a transitional object in that it is associated with the important person, often the mother.

After the death of Queen Elizabeth on 8 September 2022, many people made a connection with the comedy sketch involving Her Majesty and Paddington Bear, which had delighted the nation at the time of her Platinum Jubilee earlier in the year. This included the Queen producing a marmalade sandwich from her handbag. Paddington had explained that he kept a sandwich in his red hat, 'for emergencies'. As he produced it, the Queen responded, 'So do I.' Among the thousands of bunches of flowers laid by members of the general public in the days between the day of her death and the state funeral on 19 September were many toy Paddington Bears, as well as children's pictures of a sandwich with a reference to the sketch. These were transitional objects, a benign link to the Queen helping people to manage their sense of loss. In recognition of this, the BBC showed the film *Paddington* on the evening of 17 September and the film *Paddington 2* on the evening of 19 September, the day of Her Majesty's funeral. The link between objects, or in this case a toy, and the loss of a revered or loved person is thus shown to be a way of coping with grief in a symbolic or imaginative way, a way which can be seen as another example of creative repair.

Conclusion

In this chapter I have sought to illustrate the importance of objects that carry meaning both culturally and personally. This raises a theological question about the legitimacy of a division between the flesh and the spirit, as implied by St Paul in his Letter to the Romans: 'For those who live according to the flesh set their minds on the things of the flesh, but those who live according to the Spirit set their minds on the things of the Spirit' (Rom. 8.8). I would argue that God's Spirit can also be experienced via the meaning we give to things. Within the context of practical theology, Heather Walton has sought to challenge a binary approach to materialism. What's described as a radical incarnational theology which gives value to the material world is vulnerable to the more traditional 'faith in that which lies beyond what exists here on earth. This move is one made by Christian theology over and over again, when it discovers no way of reconciling the ambivalence of material existence with its faith in redemptive providence' (2014, p. 40). Yet when reflecting on the creative repair of things with all its evidence of redemptive potential and capacity to embody important human narrative, there seems to be an important theology of matter, a point to which I return in Chapter 9.

Notes

1 I have used BC and AD rather than BCE and CE as this is what MacGregor uses.

2 The brief accounts of these objects are drawn from Farrington, 2020.

3 See pages 16–17 for a more detailed account of Winnicott's thinking.

4 While Winnicott referred to the mother, the phrase 'good-enough' applies to the primary caregiver, who may often be the father, or a grandparent or other central figure in the child's daily life. As a psychotherapist, I aim to be a good-enough therapist and it can also apply to other helping roles, such as a pastor or nurse.

7

Regular Habits or a Rule of Life

An essential aspect of the practice of creative repair is the importance of regularity or a rhythm. This might be a weekly or monthly arrangement or even an annual festival enjoyed as an intense experience over several days. This regularity could be a part of the discipline of a rule of life, which facilitates certain qualities. These include *well-being*, *balance* and *time wisdom*. The idea of having a rule of life has become increasingly popular, not only among those who practise a particular faith, but also among others who value the spiritual dimension of their lives. Creative repair can usefully be included in a rule of life in order to embed it in the daily exercise of living the life of a faithful believer or other pursuer of spiritual practice. While my particular perspective is that of an Anglican Franciscan, the principle could also be applied not only to other Christian denominations, but also to the faithful practice of a range of religious ways of life.

The monastic tradition represents long experience of living a rule of life in community. The historian Diarmaid Mac-Culloch has recorded that from the early third century, a time when the Church first attracted very large numbers of converts in society, solitary individuals (hermits) and then groups of men and women 'took the decision to defy what they saw as an increasingly compromising involvement in the life of the Roman Empire' (2004, p. 28). This was a withdrawal in order to refocus on a Gospel-based life. Although there is no biblical precedent for monasticism as such, the recorded withdrawal of Jesus from the crowds in order to pray alone or with one or two of his disciples (for example Mark 1.35), has modelled contemplative practice for successive generations of Christians. This movement between ministry and reflective practice, modelled by Jesus, connects with both creative repair and the idea of figure/ground. By withdrawing from the crowds in order to spend time with God alone or with one or two friends, Jesus was demonstrating the need to replenish the resources poured out in his healing and teaching ministry. By moving between his leadership role with the crowds and his quiet time with God, Jesus modelled the figure/ground flexibility of a life grounded in prayer. Those living a rule of life try to follow his example.

From a historical perspective, monasticism is not without its critics, especially when practice was not congruent with the ideals and principles of key founders such as St Benedict and St Francis. Yet even though there have been times when monasticism was under attack, particularly during the dissolution of the monasteries in England and Wales in the sixteenth century, there have been subsequent revivals of the monastic life. For example, the Oxford Movement gave rise to a renewal of Anglican religious vocations in the nineteenth and twentieth centuries. At first many followed the Benedictine path and the establishment of communities based on the Franciscan rule came later. However, by the end of the last century, the historian Petà Dunstan was able to state that the Society of St Francis was the largest religious community for men in the Church of England (1997, p. xv).

Those living a consecrated life in monastic communities pray at regular times each day. At other times they work either on their monastic land or in cottage industries attached to the monastic house. Thus they combine contemplative and active ways of living out their vocation. During the early Church, there had been a tendency to view the contemplative life as eternal and superior to the temporal active life, but this was changed during the papacy of Gregory the Great (590–604). His view was that the two are complementary, with different stages of development leading to 'a union of the active and contemplative lives, not a replacement of the former by the latter' (Paffenroth, 1999, p. 3). This sense of union that balances different modes of being is one of the strengths of monasticism. It also informs the provision of facilities for rest and retreat for those visiting their houses, which 'has become a vitally important aspect of the work of most of the Anglican Religious Communities' (Stanton, 2017, p. 80).

Many monastic communities attract oblates or associates, called to follow a particular spiritual path. This usually involves a process of gradual entry or a type of noviciate and a commitment to a rule of life. There are two main ways of locating this process geographically. Most monastic houses expect oblates or associates to be attached to their particular monastic community. If the oblates or associates move to another area, their attachment is not transferable to another community. This is an expression of the Benedictine dimension of stability. By contrast, because Franciscan tertiaries are an Order in their own right, known as the Third Order, and are grouped into areas, it is easy to transfer to a different area. At the time when I identified a calling to be a Franciscan, I was married to an Army officer, which involved moving house every other year, so that it was the Third Order which offered me stability and contributed to a sense of well-being despite the disruption of frequent moves.

One of the strengths of a rule of life is that it offers an overall structure for everyday life. While particular versions of a rule of life vary, the overall aim of the founders is to live the Gospel in a more authentic way. From the sixth-century Rule of St Benedict to the twentieth-century Rule of Taizé, the founders have been concerned to help followers come closer to the Gospel. For example, Brother Roger of Taizé writes: 'This rule contains the minimum for a community to grow up in Christ and devote itself to a common service of God' (2012, p. 5). As part of their structure for everyday life, those in monastic communities are expected to have time for recreation.

For those not called to enter the religious life fully, the rule of life offers a realistic alternative to be combined with ordinary life. When St Francis encouraged the formation of the

Third Order in the thirteenth century, he recognized that many are called to serve God in the spirit of poverty, chastity and obedience in everyday life, rather than in the literal acceptance of these principles in the vows of the brothers and sisters of the First and Second Orders. The rule of the Third Order of the Society of St Francis is intended to enable the duties and conditions of daily living to be carried out in this spirit. The first aim of the Third Order is 'to make our Lord known and loved everywhere' (Society of St Francis, 2010, p. 811). The rule is Gospel-based and assumes a rhythm of daily prayer and regular attendance at the Eucharist. Tertiaries may be female or male, lay or ordained, and renew their individual rule of life annually in the presence of others. The discipline involved in trying to live out a rule of life is intended to support a holistic approach to life and can be experienced as liberating or, as the writer Esther de Waal puts it, as 'a lifeline which gives me practical help not only to hold on to my relationship with God, but also my relationship with others and myself' (1995, p. xiii). Those in ministry have a responsibility to attend to their own personal needs in order to be of service to others and thus to God. Creative repair can be most useful when it is practised routinely in everyday life. By practising it individually or in a group that meets regularly, ministers can refresh their relationships with their own creative selves. In addition, those who join others are also being refreshed by the creative mutuality due to the presence of others in the group.

Creative repair can be integrated into a rule of life. The structure of regular creative repair, whether individually or in a group setting, can complement time spent ministering to the needs of others. Further, it is my experience that the stability offered by a rule of life helps the maintenance of habits that sustain a sense of *well-being* and support a *balance* between the contemplative and active life. In addition, the idea of *time wisdom* or the way in which time may be thought about by those in ministry can greatly enhance this practice. Each of these aspects merits further consideration.

Well-being

Working in a therapeutic context, my understanding of health is often highlighted by what can go wrong in the physical, mental or psychological aspects of life. Problems are often presented as disturbances in relationships, both with others and within oneself. Often there are deep issues of identity and a quest for the meaning of life, as well as bereavement and trauma, whether in childhood, earlier adult life or more recently. This informs my belief that well-being is more than soundness of body as might be defined in a medical context and is to be found 'in every aspect of human life' (Hurding, 2013, p. 43). Beyond the balancing of psychological, social and physical resources implied by psychologists Rachel Dodge, Annette Daly, Jan Huyton and Lalage Sanders (2012, p. 230), a theological understanding demands full flourishing. This understanding is usefully summarized by Rowan Williams, who writes that 'God has made a world which *God* purposes to inhabit and which in some sense does already inhabit in that wisdom, that beauty, that order, that alluring wonder which is there in our environment' (Williams, 2007, pp. 10–11).

Well-being is complex and involves 'the incremental building of networks of human relationship and connection, self-esteem, self-belief, purpose, meaning, value and good relationships' (Webster, 2002, p. 41). Relationships are central to our experience as human beings, and while the monastic communities are particular expressions of people coming together to live a shared vision of the Christian faith, all practising Christians usually meet with others to worship God and work together to help others. Reference to relationships assumes a corporate aspect to well-being, and ministers are leaders of Christian communities. Since the days of the early Church there has been a corporate dimension to Christianity. This corporate dimension is central to a theological understanding of what it is to be a person, so to be in a healthy relationship with others is a key aspect of well-being. There is a useful difference to be made between the notions of 'individual' and 'person'. Both theologically and psychologically, the idea of a person has a stronger social implication than the idea of an individual. For Williams, the individual will always be an example of a type, whereas 'A person in Christ, a person becoming holy, is most particularly more than an "example" ... The meaning is in the utterly one-off character of their relation with the person of Jesus Christ' (2003, p. 102).

Psychologically, the idea of the social unconscious in persons has been developed in group analysis by Earl Hopper and Heim Weinberg (2011) and especially by Tom Ormay, who calls the social self the 'nos' or the 'we', which coexists with the 'I', the individual Ego. This complements the work within the theory and practice of pastoral care of both Elizabeth O'Connor (1975), who has suggested that the process of becoming is more than an individual journey, and Barbara McLure (2010), who has questioned the habitual attitude to individual and social needs as being at odds with one another. For well-being, we need relationships. Those who practise creative repair with others will, in addition to being resourced by their creative pursuit, have respite from the role of leadership and be less likely to feel that they have to do everything themselves. This will contribute to the experience of a balanced way of life.

Balance

One of the strengths of monasticism is the balance between a contemplative and an active life. As many monastic communities seek to be self-supporting, members will not only spend regular times in personal and corporate prayer, but will also work either on the land or within other aspects of their productivity. For example, the nuns of the Anglican Order of St Clare in Freeland, Oxfordshire, produce, market and distribute wafers and cards worldwide in response to regular orders. They grow vegetables and look after hens. They also have times of study, recreation and designated holidays.

Within an increasingly demanding secular work culture, the

importance of a healthy work/life balance is recognized as a way of protecting mental health against the 'potential detrimental effects of work related stress' (Mental Health Foundation, 2015). There is a discussion around the nature of ministry work: that it is part of a particular vocation and that it is not so much about who we are or what we do after ordination, but rather a 'vocational identity' grounded in our relationship with Christ (Cocksworth and Brown, 2006, pp. 5–6). This does not necessarily protect clergy from succumbing to the *zeitgeist* of busyness but does encourage reflective practice about what is being modelled for others. Joanna Collicutt, a clinical psychologist and ordained practical theologian, writing about Christian formation, suggests that there ought to be a balance 'between contemplation and action; between detachment and engagement; between hard slog and flow' (2015, p. 157). By 'flow' she is referring to Mihaly Csikszentmihalyi's notion of 'flow', his name for 'the positive aspects of human experience – joy, creativity, the process of total involvement in life' (1990, p. xi) and is the antithesis of boredom. Collicutt sees flow 'closely related to play', something which we feel 'when we do something as an end in itself, are deeply absorbed, have fun and find that our competence is increased' (2015, p. 149).

A sense of balance is more than an avoidance of extremes. Creative repair supports the ongoing ministry or pastoral work of those involved, rather than focusing on the avoidance of stress. There are various handbooks that can help the avoidance of serious stress, such as the one by Christian psychologist Kate Middleton (2015). Clergy have a particular responsibility to be stewards of their energy and resources. This involves trying to model good practice. The training and experience of psychotherapists teach that proper breaks or holidays not only meet the clinician's need to refresh her emotional and psychological energy but also give patients an opportunity to draw on their own inner resources. Regular breaks act as one check and balance against fatigue or staleness for the therapist and the danger of extended dependence on the therapist by the patient. Although clergy and other pastoral carers are not therapists, they expend psychological and emotional energy in sensitive pastoral care and this needs to be balanced by intentional and regular time off. A balanced life is helped by the capacity to move between different modes of being. The multi-faceted nature of ministry assumes that clergy are able to move in and out of different roles which often include leading worship, attending to the pastoral needs of those in their care, and fulfilling a range of administrative tasks. There is also a place for recreation and a balance that includes work, rest and play. Collicutt offers the homely metaphor that a balanced life is able to respond in a flexible way and, like a well-balanced supermarket trolley, 'can be steered in the right direction without relentlessly pulling off course down avenues of its own making' (2015, p. 142).

The capacity to move between different modes of being indicates a flexible mindset. The gestalt perspective of figure/ground is central to group analysis and helps to explain the importance of flexibility. In a working group, one person speaks and becomes the figure, while the rest of group, including the group conductor, become the ground. Another person speaks, becoming the figure, and the rest of the group become the ground. Gestalt psychotherapist Miriam Taylor describes a healthy process as one in which 'the relationship between a strong clear figure and its ground is constantly shifting and dynamic; when the process functions less well, figures are considered to be weak, stale or lacking energy' (2014, p. 42).

The words 'constantly shifting and dynamic' imply strength and flexibility. Helpfully, the theologian David Ford distinguishes between a balance between extremes, a way of restraining impulse and excess, and 'a balancing which is dynamic and is always on the point of overbalancing as it moves ... a picture of desires which are being shaped by one overwhelming desire ... the movement that integrates and balances all the others' (2012, p. 27). He writes in the context of discerning vocation or of responding to God's invitation to desire what God desires. This sense of the foundational desire of God also connects with the rule of life because it offers a flexible structure within which to move in and out of different modes, all of which are expressions of serving God in prayer and practice. The flexibility offered by the gestalt perspective of figure/ground is central to the group-analytic understanding of what happens in groups. One way of thinking about figure and ground is, for example, what we hold in the front of our mind and what is going on in the background. Applying this to ministry, the figure (in this case the individual clergy person) is also part of the ground (their local worshipping community; their denomination; their culture; their social group). All that is expressed in a group 'is the foreground, the figure of a process which in its totality comprises the whole group and on the ground of which meaning becomes defined, interpretation springs to life' (Foulkes, 1986, pp. 131–2). Applied to ministry, clergy are often bound to be the figure in the foreground when in a public role but could be resourced when they are able to be part of the ground in their practice of creative repair in a group context, as demonstrated by the experience of Steve.

Steve

Steve had been in ministry for five years. Before being ordained he had regularly played the tuba in his local brass band, enjoying the weekly practices and the occasional performances for local civic events. After his ordination, he moved diocese to serve his title as a curate and didn't get round to finding a local brass band in his new area. The challenge of learning all the skills and competencies of his ordained and public role as well as completing the initial ministry education (IME) left little time for recreational activities. Having a study day, as well as a weekly day off, meant that he did not really think about his tuba playing as a necessary way of resourcing himself.

A year later, after Steve had completed his curacy and been appointed incumbent of another parish, he began to feel the loneliness of being in a leadership role. He remembered how much he had enjoyed playing his tuba in his local brass band

and looked for one which was outside his parish, but within easy commuting distance. As it happened, the one he found was short of a tuba player. He prioritized the day of the weekly band practice so that it did not clash with parish meetings. When he met with his spiritual director after two years in the new post, Steve reflected on the difference that joining the new brass band had made. Not only had he made a new group of friends, but he enjoyed being under the bandmaster's baton and being just one of the players. Playing his tuba was also an emotional release and he returned home refreshed each week.

Reflection

This is a perfect example of creative repair in a group setting. Like many newly ordained clergy, Steve had felt an obligation to give up many aspects of his past life. Although he had been taught about the importance of self-care in his ministry training, he had understood that in terms of a day off a week and a regular retreat or quiet day. His previous enjoyment of playing in his local brass band had slipped into the past and he had not been helped to see how relevant it was for his ongoing need to sustain his ministry. His curacy had involved a study day each week and this had supplemented the weekly day off. Also, he was not the incumbent, so that he was in a supportive role. His Training Incumbent had been rather intense and serious and would probably not have approved of brass bands, except perhaps on Remembrance Sunday. By reclaiming this important aspect of his past identity, Steve not only ensured a weekly evening off, but also joined the band as an experienced if somewhat rusty tuba player and was immediately welcomed and thanked for joining them. It was the custom of the band to go for a drink after practice, so that he also began to have a social life outside his parish. He enjoyed making music with the band and his wife commented that he came home in a good mood. Using the figure/ground metaphor, he moved from being the figure in his ministry context to being part of the ground in the band, except for rare occasions when the tuba had a solo. By prioritizing the weekly band practice, Steve also modelled to his ministry team and parishioners that he was actively taking care of his own recreational needs. The weekly rhythm protected his creative repair and his wish not to let down the rest of the band helped him to attend regularly. It also helped to balance the intensity of pastoral work.

Time wisdom

The practice of creative repair benefits from a flexible approach to different roles. One factor which can obstruct a person's intentional commitment to time off can be the prevalence of busyness among clergy and other Christian pastors, including volunteers. The fact is that many clergy have too much to do, and this can be a burden that can seem unmanageable. A sustainable approach to this involves more than a work/life balance or time management. It demands another way of thinking about time.

Time is a complex notion. Human beings exist at a particular time in history, time which is measured chronologically. At the same time, Christians, as followers of Jesus, are called to be *in* the world yet not *of* the world (John 17.16). This implies a sense of God's time or *kairos*, so there is a paradox that, while being engaged in the minute-by-minute, hour-by-hour ongoing experience of measured time or *chronos*, Christians are invited to view time sacramentally. De Caussade wrote that 'the will of God is manifest in each moment, an immense ocean which the heart only fathoms insofar as it overflows with faith, trust and love' (1981, p. 82). This sacramental view of time has to be reconciled with the minister's practical need to manage a huge number of tasks, and it demands more than time-management techniques.

One response to the problem of time pressure and the experience of busyness among clergy has been developed in Stephen Cherry's idea of *time wisdom* (2012). He suggests that 'time wise' people are able to embrace both *chronos* and *kairos*. Ministers need to become aware of their 'temporal personality' (2012, p. 101), noticing and understanding their experience of time. 'Time wisdom' is developed slowly and is helped by a notion of 'timescape', by which Cherry intends an analogy with landscape.

Such a 'timescape' will be marked by three qualities: first, for some, it is part of the greater whole of the timescape of the Church. The rhythm of corporate and eucharistic worship, connected with the first day of the week and daily morning and evening prayer, allows for regular engagement with scripture, sacrament and prayer, and brings a calming structure to daily life. This resonates with the monastic life, with its rhythm of the daily offices said several times a day. At least one day a week for rest, recovery and leisure balances more demanding times and allows for the flexibility when needed to respond to occasional crises.

Second, a sustainable 'timescape' is realistic and takes account of the particular life stage and personal commitments of the clergy person. These may vary over time, perhaps in response to the demands of family life or to an evolving stage in ministry or changing state of physical health. If clergy are able to adapt to the particular challenges of their own life stage while in public ministry, they are modelling sustainable ministry to those whom they serve.

The third quality of 'timescape' is that of flexibility. Cherry comments that 'when for whatever reason you pull it out of shape, it slowly reverts to a healthy and sustainable form' (2012, p. 104). This flexibility of mind regarding time connects in a figurative sense with the idea of figure/ground. Just as the clergy person moves in and out of different modes of being according to the different roles required, so a flexible approach to time allows for an ebb and flow in response to the particular needs of the present moment.

If clergy are able to practise creative repair in a group context, they will increase their sense of well-being by balancing the requirements of ministry with their own need to renew their creative energy. By showing flexibility both in their experience of 'timescape' and their capacity to move in and out of leadership role, they can sustain their practice of ministry. Although they may not live out a formal rule of life, the monastic model suggests that regular habits of balancing work and leisure, solitude and community, enable the elasticity needed to respond to the variable demands of ministry.

8

Resilience and Creative Repair

Resilience is generally understood as the capacity to bounce or spring back from pressure. If practised routinely, creative repair can contribute to resilience. Habits make a difference, as do a sense of balance and a thoughtful use of time. Resilience also connects with a sense of meaning and purpose. For clergy it helps to be part of an organization that looks beyond itself to a wish to bring more people into what Jesus referred to as the Kingdom of God. Recent writers such as Diane Coutu and Justine Allain-Chapman and before them Viktor E. Frankl can help to identify factors that contribute to resilience.

Coutu on resilience

Resilience has been described as 'one of the great puzzles of human nature, like creativity or the religious instinct' (Coutu, 2017, p. 5). It is a widely used word and is something that you can only recognize when reflecting later on a particularly challenging period of life. In a short book published by the Harvard Business School, Diane Coutu has helpfully considered three aspects of resilience that surfaced from her research, and that offer an initial framework for the puzzle of resilience.

First, Coutu highlights the importance of 'facing down reality' (p. 11). There is a common view that resilience stems from an optimistic nature. For this to be true there needs to be an absence of distortion. Whereas T. S. Eliot famously commented that 'humankind cannot bear very much reality' (1959, p. 14), an essential quality of resilience is the capacity to face reality.

Over-optimism can be a handicap in stressful situations. Resilient people have a down-to-earth view of the need for survival. Those who are in denial put themselves at risk. Facing reality means making preparations 'to act in ways that allow us to endure and survive extraordinary hardship. We train ourselves how to survive before the fact' (Coutu, 2017, p. 15).

Second, what Coutu describes as 'the search for meaning' (p. 15) involves being able to make meaning during difficult or even terrible times rather than taking a victim stance. It is the capacity to see oneself in perspective, to ask 'Why not me' rather than the subjective lament 'Why me?' Taking inspiration from the experience of Viktor E. Frankl, survivor of the Holocaust, she writes that this 'dynamic of meaning making ... is the way resilient people build bridges from present-day hardships to a fuller, better-constructed future' (p. 17). Coutu cites Frankl's invention of 'meaning therapy', a humanistic therapy technique that helps individuals to make the kinds of decisions that will create significance in their lives. He created imaginary goals for himself in order to rise above the sufferings of the moment. After talking to a fellow-prisoner about their wives, he had a turning-point moment during a brutal march on which guards bullied slow walkers. As he stumbled on, 'my mind clung to my wife's image, imagining it with uncanny acuteness. I heard her answering me, saw her smile, her frank and encouraging look. Real or not, her look was then more luminous than the sun which was beginning to rise' (Frankl, 1959, edn 2011, p. 30). This experience gave him profound insight into the power of love: 'A thought transfixed me: for the first time in my life I saw the truth as it is set into song by so many poets, proclaimed as the final truth by so many thinkers. The truth – that love is the ultimate and the highest goal to which man can aspire' (p. 30). This experience, which gave Frankl a way of surviving the awful conditions of the camp, taught him that his imagination had the power to lift his spirits. By visualizing his wife's presence at a time when he did not even know whether or not she was alive, he re-entered his loving relationship with her and through that reached a profound and universal understanding of the meaning of love. It was the beginning of the thinking that was to inspire him to create what he later called logotherapy, defined as 'a meaning-centred therapy' (p. 80).

According to Coutu, since finding meaning in one's environment is such an important aspect of resilience, the most successful organizations and people have strong value systems (2017, p. 20). This puts religious organizations in a strong position and may help to explain why clergy are particularly vulnerable if they experience a crisis of belief, because they can feel as if they are betraying the institution of the Church, unless their approach to faith is one that embraces doubt as part of the spiritual journey. However, regarding the survival of institutions, Coutu comments: 'Resilience is neither ethically good nor bad. It is merely the skill and the capacity to be robust under conditions of enormous stress and change' (p. 22).

The third aspect of Coutu's useful analysis of resilience is 'ritualized ingenuity' or what she cites the French anthropologist Claude Lévi-Strauss as having called 'bricolage'. This is the ability to make do with whatever is at hand. 'Bricolage ... can be defined as a kind of inventiveness, an ability to improvise a solution to a problem without proper or obvious tools or materials' (Coutu, 2017, p. 24). However, it is not the same as 'unbridled creativity'. Discipline is required, such as useful habits. One example is the habit of putting keys in the same place. There is a balance between ingenuity and the value of some rules and regulations in order to ensure and protect consistency.

Coutu concludes that being lucky is not the same as being resilient: 'Resilience is a reflex – a way of facing and understanding the world – that is deeply etched into a person's mind and soul. Resilient people and companies face reality with staunchness, make meaning of hardship instead of crying out in despair, and improvise solutions from thin air' (p. 30).

The focus of Coutu's work has been the resilience of organizations and she has seen it as an ethically neutral quality. A writer who has explored resilience in the context of ministry is

Justine Allain-Chapman. In her book *Resilient Pastors* (2012), she has highlighted the role of adversity in healing and growth. She set out to answer two questions: The first is 'How can I help others to be strengthened during difficulties in life?' The second is 'How can I cope when I'm overwhelmed with the demands of helping others?'

Allain-Chapman on resilience

Allain-Chapman explores the desert as metaphor. There are three stages 'which describe the process of growing in resilience and do so with attention given to struggle, self and relationships' (p. 57). The stages are embracing the desert, encountering God and the self, and altruistic living and pastoral responsibility.

Embracing the desert is 'acknowledging the need to survive brought about by the physical and psychological vulnerability of being alone in a barren landscape, be it real or metaphorical' (p. 54). There is nowhere to hide, and this connects with Coutu's 'facing down reality'. Allain-Chapman spent eight days in the Sinai Peninsula while on sabbatical leave, whereas others may spend time on a rocky island or in a rural setting. The point for the retreatant is to stay in touch with that vulnerability and be open to whatever can be learned from the experience. It seems that 'certain truths can be learned...only as one is sufficiently emptied, frightened, or confused' (p. 54).

This leads to the second movement of resilience: *encountering the self and God*, which comes from the recognition that one's vulnerability can be experienced as integration and growth in wholeness. Often people who have had near-death experiences or those who are facing terminal illness look hard at their priorities and work out what are the essentials in life. Those who enter the desert may seek an experience of adversity or a voluntary stripping of self or 'a purging that demands a deep sense of relinquishment' (p. 55).

The third movement of the desert metaphor is that of

altruistic living and pastoral responsibility. Allain-Chapman indicates that this is present in the biblical desert narratives and is described in the texts of fourth- and fifth-century desert Christians, especially in the relationship between elder and disciple. One of the pastor's tasks is to help people to 'embrace the desert' by confronting the reality of their situation. It involves developing a capacity to live beyond themselves, while not neglecting appropriate self-care.

This could be linked to Frankl's search for meaning, which comes from his own experience. A pastor who has not confronted her or his own struggle will not be able to do this with authenticity. For Henri Nouwen, this may come in the form of personal or professional loneliness, the latter being particularly difficult. For Nouwen, 'This is a very hard call, because for a minister who is committed to forming a community of faith, loneliness is a very painful wound which is easily subject to denial and neglect. But once the pain is accepted and understood, a denial is no longer necessary, and ministry can become a healing service' (Nouwen, 1979, edn 1994, p. 87). The loneliness to which Nouwen refers can be eased by the pastor's membership of a group experience of creative repair. While resilience may be developed in various ways, if it is to be sustained beyond crises it needs to be routinely supported by healthy habits of renewal.

Pandemic as desert and resilience

The first two years of the Covid pandemic that began in 2020 involved exclusion from everyday life, as periodic lockdowns affected all substantial gatherings whether indoors or outdoors. This impacted both on regular worship and occasional offices, especially weddings and funerals, and certainly met the criterion of metaphorical desert. During this time, many ministry teams set up phone hubs and began streaming services. As lockdowns eased, many churches continued to stream main services. The many innovations were evidence of Coutu's third observation of resilience, that of 'ritualized ingenuity'.

Of course, this came at a price and many clergy reported feelings of exhaustion. While the desert involves struggle that can enhance spiritual growth, it is a fine line for the most robust of natures. For those with mental health conditions, the situation can tip them from management of their symptoms to overload and crisis. For any of us, a cluster of losses can overload our capacity to process each loss and can develop into trauma. During the first two years of the pandemic, clergy concerns included the constantly changing situation and how to minister in a crisis with no gatherings. In such circumstances, it is even more important that clergy identify pastimes that resource rather than drain them and see these as necessary self-care. Such pastimes should be in the diary and be part of their regular spiritual disciplines. It is helpful for clergy not to be 'on duty' when doing them. It is important that they regularly review the balance of ministry and self-care. 'Going the extra mile' cannot be routinely sustained, or else it is a shortcut to burnout, which serves no one.

At a workshop during a clergy conference in 2022, I invited participants to name what had helped them to survive the previous two years. Answers varied from the habit of walking the dog, to reading a novel, time with family and resuming former pastimes, such as playing a musical instrument or enjoying hand sewing. After some teaching about creative repair and an experience in the here and now, feedback indicated the importance of being given permission to practise creative repair as a matter of good stewardship and of obedience to the God who wants us to flourish. The need to set dates in the diary to protect regular time as part of spiritual practice was recognized. As it was an in-person group experience, what cannot be recorded verbally was the sense of mutuality and creative thinking, so absent during the pandemic.

I work routinely with NHS staff teams, conducting reflective practice groups and supervising those working in palliative care. Although we were able to work online, which certainly helped to mitigate against the feelings of isolation, one of the themes was lament for the loss of casual encounters, such as meeting in corridors or around the kettle or water cooler. Old assumptions could no longer be taken for granted and heads could not be popped round the door of a colleague's office. It became clear that these sporadic encounters were a crucial part of everyday resilience. Applying Coutu's ideas, there was no shortage of the capacity to face down reality or need to search for meaning. It was the third aspect of resilience, the capacity for 'ritualized ingenuity', that helped practitioners to resource themselves while grieving for the loss of face-to-face meetings. More use was made of phone contact, and informal walking meetings with another colleague helped to reduce the sense of isolation.

Using Allain-Chapman's criteria, although the desert metaphor certainly applied to the pandemic experience, especially during periods of lockdown, the lack of agency made it harder for people to benefit from any sense of it being an opportunity to embrace the desert. Nevertheless, many people took the opportunity to review their priorities, and in terms of altruistic living, the increase in people's concern for their neighbours was one of the outcomes.

Grayson Perry

As indicated in Chapter 2 and worth repeating here, twice during periods of lockdown, the ceramicist Grayson Perry and his wife Philippa, a psychotherapist, opened their home to *Grayson's Art Club*, a television series in which themes were developed and the general public were invited to submit artwork on the theme of the week. Just as Gareth Malone has sought to cross imagined boundaries of elitism when gathering and rehearsing his choirs in a variety of settings, Perry has intentionally extended the invitation to be creative to people in every context, with assumptions of inclusivity.

During each programme he would invite a celebrity to have a go at creating something and interviewed those who had created his favourite artefacts. After each series an exhibition was arranged so that the general public could visit and admire the chosen artworks and perhaps be inspired to be creative themselves.

Resilience and creative repair

Clergy stress is becoming an increasingly worrying concern. Stress that continues unattended over a substantial period of time can lead to burnout. This stress is partly due to the variety of skills and demands that characterize ministry and partly a result of a strong work ethic and the reality that ministry is a never-ending process. There is usually a limited amount of paid assistance, perhaps in a parish office, but most of the potential assistance comes from volunteers. If the clergy person is vulnerable to the 'I'm in charge' approach to ministry, coupled with a relentless work ethic, this can exacerbate the level of stress and promote the likelihood of burnout. It is essential to work in teams, even if they have to be virtual ones some of the time, and face the reality that none of us is indispensable. As Allain-Chapman has put it, 'Resilience is built by healthy, supportive and mutual relationships' (2012, p. 126).

Giving up the idea of being indispensable involves seeing that the whole community is involved in ministry. It may mean redesigning structures in a parish, so that they do not all revolve around the vicar or leading pastor. This will involve many conversations, a method highlighted by Allain-Chapman: 'Conversation as a model has many strengths ... lies at the centre of human and pastoral encounters ... works with the hiddenness of human personality, thus pointing to the need to express theology in terms of story, metaphor, image and symbol' (p. 8). This creative approach to theology encourages each person to reflect on the meaning of faith and the ways in which it can be expressed in action.

During the pandemic, it became necessary for worship leaders to develop new ways of expressing faith, denied the usual assumptions of gatherings in a building with some form of musical accompaniment. It demanded what Coutu called 'ritualized ingenuity' in order to keep things going, and drew on the skills of those who were at home in technology. Meanwhile the hybrid approach of a mixture of face-to-face meetings and virtual meetings has become widespread, and few churches have returned solely to pre-pandemic practices.

While this may have drawn more people into the weekly tasks of enabling liturgy, for many clergy it has raised the expectations of congregations and therefore the danger of being overloaded. Resilience relies on regular habits and the definition of creative repair can be widened to include such activities as gardening and cooking.

Conclusion

If resilience is something of a puzzle, then we have some clues to help us to solve it. Of the various clues presented by Coutu and Allain-Chapman, the search for meaning emerges as a central dimension. Reading Frankl exposes us to the most traumatic events of the last century. His observations of the behaviour of his fellow-captives informed his radical view of the importance of aspiring to some vision, some glimpse of life outside the camp with its relentless brutality in order to survive against impossible odds. Fortunately, most of us are not called to deal with such extreme events. Yet we each have to face the challenge to survive from the moment we are conceived. If we have a sense of the preciousness of life, whether helped by our original family or others who have supported us, we have a chance to engage our creative selves. For those with a religious faith, creative repair can be understood as part of the gift of life itself. In the next chapter, I will consider the theology of creative repair.

9

Towards a Theology of Creative Repair

Why do we need a theology of creative repair? Alister McGrath has argued for the centrality of theology in the provocative title of his book *What's the Point of Theology?* (2022). Reflecting on the impact that his conversion to Christianity made on his world view, he writes: 'No longer did I see the world as "nature"; I saw it as God's creation. No longer did I see people as socioeconomic units; I saw them as individuals bearing the image of God' (p. 12). I believe that as Creator of our universe, God is implicitly present in all human creativity. Those involved in the creative arts may be seen as co-creators with God.

George Herbert

As well as being a musician, my priest father loved the poems of George Herbert. Now that I have his copy of the collected works, I encounter not only the poet himself but also the text which my father perused throughout his life: an example of the creative repair of things. Poetry has the gift of expressing a lot in a few words. McGrath points out that Herbert could teach us two ways of doing theology in the third verse of his poem 'The Elixir' (the basis of the popular hymn 'Teach me my God and King', as set to music by Sandys).

A man that looks on glasse,
On it may stay his eye;
Or if he pleaseth, through it passe,
And then the heaven espie.
(Herbert, 1945/1959, p. 184)

McGrath suggests that it is possible to look *at* things, such as the Christian doctrine of Creation, or to look *through* Christian doctrines 'to allow Christian theology to become a window to viewing ourselves and the world. He wants us to *use* theology so that we can develop a deeper and richer engagement with our world and see it afresh' (McGrath, pp. 13–14). If we use theology in this way, it becomes clearer that creative repair is a lens for one aspect of theology, that of creativity in practice as practitioners become co-creators with the divine ongoing creativity.

One of the functions of the regular practice of creative repair is to engage with the creative arts in a way that resources and refreshes the one who engages with them. It is an opportunity to have respite from the daily tasks of ministry and other pastoral work and become absorbed in God's co-creators, whether through poetry (including songwriting), painting (whether in an art class or through a visit to a gallery), theatre (whether as performers or audience), or music in its widest expressions (whether through playing an instrument, singing in a choir or going to a concert or gig). By going through the 'glasse', we may heaven 'espie'.

Writing as vocation

This also applies to writers. In her work on the writing methods in theological reflection, Heather Walton has argued for the careful craft of writing in a theological context to be just as important as the craft of sermon writing:

I have written this chapter in the same way as I preach. I have shaped and formed and laboured over it in the same way that I think a sermon is crafted. It is a human process but it is also one in which we can recognize, as we may in many other human labours, our participation in the work of God. This is my job, and it is my calling. (Walton, 2014, p. 20)

Walton's reference to her calling or vocation speaks to the many ways in which we may be called or re-called to serve God, whether in ministry, or in the helping professions or in writing for the benefit of a wider readership.

God as Creator

In our creative, pastoral listening, especially to those who are experiencing loss and bereavement, we are pouring ourselves out when being alongside others. Often there is little that we can say or do, but the capacity to be present, representing God as Christ loving his neighbour, is itself of enormous help to those who are grieving. Afterwards, we need to resource ourselves by making ourselves available to another aspect of God, in particular to God as Creator. Thus, we *repair* ourselves creatively.

If there is a parallel between God's creativity and our human obedience to the creative imperative, then our creative activity may offer a shortcut to divine presence. In this we have the example of some religious artists and all icon painters. Coming out of Byzantine culture and life, icons are associated with the Orthodox tradition of Christianity. In the words of St John of Damascus, 'icons are theology not only in words but images' (quoted in a handout given by Sister Esther OSB during SAOMC ministry training, 2000, cited in Holmes, 2011, p. 77). For icon painters, prayer is expressed in the act of painting. One of the outcomes of the Iconoclast controversy, which raged from the early eighth to mid-ninth centuries and permitted the veneration of icons, was that certain principles were established, including the value of icons as an enhancement of the doctrine of Creation.

Icons safeguard the spirit-bearing potentialities of all material things. It is a profound example of the theology of matter, to which I referred in Chapter 6. John of Damascus wrote: 'I shall not cease to honour matter, for it was through matter that my salvation came to pass ... Do not despise matter, for it is not despicable: nothing is despicable that God has made' ('In Defence of the Holy Icons' from 'The Spirituality of the Icon' handout at a Core MA Module taught by Jane Leach, 2002–2003). Walton has drawn on the work of the Franciscan Sister and theologian Ilia Delio in her critique of the traditional binary life/matter Christological view of the material world:

> For Scotus and Bonaventure, the universe is the external embodiment of the inner Word of God ... Bonaventure writes that in his transfiguration Christ shares existence with all things: with the stones he shares existence, with the plants he shares life, with animals he shares sensation ... In his human nature, he stated, 'Christ embraces something of every creature in himself'. (Delio cited in Walton, 2014, p. 40)

While icon painting is perhaps the ultimate form of creative repair, all human creativity is implied in my discussion and may perhaps be thought of as God-breathed. I perceive God to be the Creator of the universe who has created human beings and given them the freedom to respond to him or not. It would therefore be inappropriate to say that human creativity is of the same order. As it is impossible to define God, who is beyond description, in anything other than an approximate way, it can only be with a sense of humility and 'not-knowing' that we can try to apprehend divine creativity via our understanding of the experience of human creativity.

As there is often little that we can say or do when we are alongside those who are experiencing loss and bereavement, the ministry of presence, being alongside, often wordlessly, is not to be underrated. This practice of being receptive in the pastoral encounter has its corollary in our capacity to be receptive to God's healing grace through the arts. By allowing ourselves to be drawn into the creative arts, we hand ourselves over so that God can replenish us. R. S. Thomas has put this eloquently in his poem 'The Flower' (1993, p. 280). Addressing God, he reflects on how God gave him so much in response to his request for riches. In order to take all this in he knows that he must withdraw and give himself totally to the experience of God's regard. He ends the poem: 'The soul grew in me, filling me with its fragrance.'

Creative repair in the here and now

One of the features of the many workshops on creative repair that I have conducted over the years has been to give the participants the opportunity for a here and now experience of being lost in a piece of music while being free to wander around the room and look at various pieces of art, both original and reproduction. The piece I have usually chosen is from the compact disc by Howard Goodall *Enchanted Voices* (2009).

Challenged to write a new piece every month while he was Classic FM's Composer-in-Residence, Goodall chose to set the Beatitudes to music. As there were only eight mentioned in the Sermon on the Mount recorded in St Matthew's Gospel, Goodall invented four more beatitudes: for those that are cared for; those that care for others; those that are lonely and those who are stateless. The first two are set before the eight biblical beatitudes and the second two afterwards. The first setting, for those that are cared for, is a perfect representation in music of creative repair, as it sets some Latin text and includes the English words: 'Blessed are they that are cared for, a light will be shone on their path.' The music is exquisite and lasts for a full seven minutes. Whatever the musical tastes and preferences of the workshop participants, because they are mostly familiar with music in liturgy they usually experience a few minutes of transcendence. The mood changes and after a short period of silence they reflect on their experience and where their minds wandered during the seven minutes. Many of them resolve that it *is* possible to create time for such opportunities to resource themselves routinely, if only for a few minutes in a busy day.

Other feedback from workshops with clergy has highlighted the importance of being affirmed in the practice of creative repair. For example: 'Giving myself permission and the chance to enjoy flourishing and resilience through deliberate sabbaths, relaxation, engaging with activities completely different to ministry work. Not feeling guilty taking up these things that refresh and renew me.' Refreshment and renewal are key outcomes of creative repair, which often includes an encounter with beauty.

The philosopher John Armstrong has written of *The Secret Power of Beauty* (2004/5). He ends by citing two examples in western culture: Mahler's song-cycle *Das Lied von der Erde* and Thomas Mann's *Death in Venice*. Both are associated with dying: 'Mahler and Mann each place the final recognition of beauty at the most emotive, but least productive moment of life – the last', and Armstrong adds: 'The hope of culture has always been, in effect, to improve our timing. That we might be in a position to appreciate beauty more fully not when life comes to an end, but when we close a book' (2005, p. 164). Many Christians would want to place this in the context of the beauty of God.

The beauty of God

Richard Harries has long been an ambassador for the arts and their expression of the beauty of God: 'For without an affirmation of beauty there can in the end be no faith and no God worth our love' (1993, p. 1). Writing over a period of more than 30 years, he has worked to embrace a broader Christian view of the place of the arts in the nature of God than is sometimes acknowledged by both Protestant and

Catholic sources. Speaking of the 100th anniversary of T. S. Eliot's *The Waste Land*, and the 100th anniversary in book form of James Joyce's *Ulysses* in a regular contribution to BBC Radio Four's Thought for the Day, Harries commented: 'What is noteworthy about both works is how they draw on the past. Joyce's novel is a conscious parallel of Homer's *Odyssey* and Eliot's poem is steeped in literary references. Great literature lives on in all kinds of ways' (broadcast on 24 June 2022 and cited with permission). After reflecting on the power of words in Christianity and Judaism, he added that great literature tells the truth about things and concluded:

> Serious writers are in the end in the business of moral and spiritual truth. They seek to feel more deeply, think more clearly and imagine more widely than most of us. They can refresh the language and help shape our whole culture. (Thought for the Day, 24 June 2022).

Whether or not they espouse a particular religious faith, by their obedience to the creative impulse and their artistic vocation, writers, artists and musicians are co-creators with the divine and by engaging with their works we can resource ourselves.

Transformation and flourishing

In the opening pages of *Wounds that Heal* (Williams, 2007), Rowan Williams suggests (p. 5) that the whole business of theology is to trace how God transforms flesh, how God makes flesh inhabited, by creating living relationship within himself. He goes on to say:

> Ultimately it's not just that God has made a world to be inhabited, but that God has made a world which *God* purposes to inhabit and which in some sense God does already inhabit in that wisdom, that beauty, that order, that alluring wonder which is there in our environment ... [The] pivotal moment is when God fully and unequivocally inhabits that life which

is Jesus of Nazareth, that death and that resurrection which belong to Jesus of Nazareth and which make all the difference to your body and mine so that our own inhabiting of the world changes. (pp. 10–11)

Williams was giving the inaugural Hildegard Lecture in 2003, so it seems odd that, 20 years later, these words still come over as radical in their implication as expressed a little later:

The Good News the gospel tells us is that, first of all the world is inhabited by its maker; second, that the maker of the world has made it possible for us to inhabit the world more fully, more deeply, more joyfully than we could ever have possibly imagined. (p. 11)

This seems to offer a clear theological justification for the need to engage fully with the creation and, I would argue, in particular with the creative arts as a living expression of God's continuing creativity.

The idea of *shalom* in Judaism indicates full flourishing and it comes to my mind when Williams answers the question: Is theology a story of healing? Drawing on Vladimir Lossky's suggestion that you look at holy people if you want to know what the Holy Spirit looks like, he explains: 'You look at inhabited faces, faces that stopped being flesh in the negative sense ... the untenanted, the empty space, where relation doesn't happen, the spark doesn't kindle, where there is a kind of deadness and a kind of isolation which makes us less than human' (Williams, 2007, p. 13). He reminds us that we learn to live in heaven only when we learn to live on earth in the here and now and inhabit the space that God has given us.

This idea of inhabiting the space which God has given us seems to me to be entirely consistent with the idea of creative repair. If the priest, faith leader, pastoral carer or parent is alongside another in a receptive, incarnational way, accompanying the other in pain or grief, then it is essential for her or him to replenish the emotional, psychological and spiritual resources that have been thus poured out. While it is true that some encounters are themselves mutually replenishing, unless they are in the habit of self-observation caregivers may not discern those encounters that drain them. Also, they often go from one task to another.

Drawing on my work with some clergy who get run down, in my clinical judgement an idealized view of the role contributes to their fatigue and a culture of endless self-sacrifice justifies the ignoring of fatigue. Two participants in my earlier research indicated that this slowly accrues to burnout and can actually mean that the pastor is obliged to go on sick leave and therefore be totally unavailable to others.

Williams gives a hint of one of the causes of this when he mentions the role of habit. Considering the notion of sin, as seen by St Paul in Galatians 5, he compares it to uninhabited flesh: 'the flesh used in a meaningless, destructive or isolating way, and *our simple habits*, things that keep us prisoner in our own relation with God, the things that set a ceiling on our growth towards God' (Williams, 2007, p. 9, my italics) have a lot to do with that sense of uninhabited flesh. This role of habit is one of the core themes of most psychological help. If we can change some of our habits, then we have a chance of opening ourselves up to fresh vision, fresh confidence in our ability to respond each day to the opportunities for growth and development. As outlined in Chapter 7, establishing regular rhythms and habits can help to anchor the practice of creative repair and thus act to sustain ministry in a way that prevents burnout.

Practical theology

There are various ways of exploring theology and the discipline of practical theology has been the context of the research that I have conducted in order to test out my theory of creative repair. Practical theology has been described by Bonnie Miller-McLemore as referring to at least four enterprises: a *discipline* among scholars; a faith *activity* among believers; a *method* or way of understanding or analysing theology in practice; and a *curricular area* for those training in ministry (Miller-McLemore, 2012, p. 5). The four different views are 'connected and interdependent' (p. 5). This description recognizes that practical theology, an evolving discipline, is multivalent and can be conceived broadly.

The fourfold description allowed me to locate my doctoral study in a helpfully broad framework. Each of the enterprises matches an aspect of that study. First, in an obvious way, as part of a doctoral programme the study sought to contribute to the work of a growing community of scholars whose task is 'to support and sustain' the other three enterprises (Miller-McLemore, 2012, p. 5). As my study invited clergy participants to reflect on their ministry and regular practice of creative repair, it could be included in Miller-McLemore's second category of practical theology as a faith activity among believers. As a method for studying theology in practice, my study, focusing as it did on the ministry of Anglican clergy, sought to understand and analyse 'theology in practice used by religious leaders' (p. 5). This third category embraces both theory (or methodology) and particular methods. Among the particular methods described in Part II of Miller-McLemore's companion to practical theology, those which I considered or used included the case study and psychological theory (Shipani, 2012, pp. 91–101; Butler, 2012, pp. 102–11). Fourth, if my findings were to indicate that clergy benefit from the practice of creative repair in a group, then this study would have curricular implications for both initial ministerial training and continuing ministerial development. One of the aims of this book is to help the process of disseminating the outcomes of my research in the hope that it will inform future clergy selection and training and continuing ministerial education.

Swinton and Mowat's suggestion that practical theology combines the faithful performance of the Gospel with embodiment in human experience (2006, pp. 4–5) is, in my view, too narrow. Their apparent restriction of practical theology to a Christian context has been contested by Pattison who takes a broader perspective. His view is that 'God is to be found in all people and places and can be learned about best often at the edges of orthodox religious communities and thought systems' (2007, p. 18). This echoes Williams's suggestion, cited earlier but worth repeating here, that 'God has made a world which *God* purposes to inhabit and which in some sense God does already inhabit' (2007, p. 10) and affirms my belief that practical theology ought to be conceived broadly.

Practical theology is a discipline which can facilitate theological reflection on ministerial practice and enable practitioners to 'draw belief and action closer together' (Cameron and Duce, 2013, p. xi). Within the Christian context, without wanting to downgrade the importance of other areas of practical theology, my particular interest has been in the ministry of clergy and other church leaders. This is both for their sake and because of their importance as role models as leaders of their congregations and of Christian culture.

Since the 1980s, practical theology has joined other professions in valuing the Aristotelian idea of *phronesis* or practical wisdom as an important source of knowledge (Graham, 1996, p. 7; Miller-McLemore, 2012, p. 2). Practical theologians such as Browning, Ballard and others broadened the understanding of practical theology to embrace congregational studies. A congregation in crisis might re-examine the sacred texts, engaging in a dialogue with changing practices. Moving from practice to theological reflection and back to practice has opened up new perspectives. Informed by the Christian tradition and other sources of knowledge, this has been described as a '"correlational" process of reflection leading to transformation' (Graham, Walton and Ward, 2005, p. 128).

My training and experience as a group analyst and psychodynamic psychotherapist working with groups and individuals have been a major source of internalized knowledge in my studies. Both the psychological understanding gained through this discipline, and the clinically focused routine of reflective practice that such work involves, are key sources that I have brought to my thinking. Reflective practice is increasingly part of many disciplines, and part of my work as a group analyst has been to facilitate reflective practice with staff teams in the NHS. In the case of one group, my co-facilitator was the hospital chaplain. Although I am employed as a clinician and draw on psychological theory to frame my work, as a Christian I also see all of my work through a theological lens, albeit one whose theological expression is implicit rather than explicit. As an ordained group analyst, I believe that practical theology has been the ideal discipline within which to locate my research, given its interdisciplinary nature (Woodward and Pattison, 2000, p. 15).

Liturgy, theology and the arts

In recent decades, a growing interest in the links between liturgy, theology and the arts has led to the development of university departments in the English-speaking world. Hilary Davies has described her experience of a three-day conference in 2022, organized by the Centre for Catholic Studies at Durham University and the University of Notre Dame's London Global Gateway, in association with *The Tablet* and the Jesuit Church at Farm Street, London. It included a visit to the National Gallery to see four Bellini paintings to back up one of the talks. An evening Mass was followed by a performance of Messiaen's *Quatuor pour la fin du temps*, scored for clarinet, violin, cello and piano, a twentieth-century masterpiece conceived and performed during the Second World War. Davies comments that: 'Messiaen's ultimate aim is to give expression to the ineffable: as the violin ascends into silence in the final bars, liturgy and place have become one in a piece of music that has carried us to the edge of time and space, into the presence of God.' She concludes: 'the riches offered by this interdisciplinary meeting are set to reverberate in all manner of creative ways in the minds of those who were lucky enough to take part' (2022, p. 5).

Conclusion

For Christians, the example of Jesus Christ sets the pattern for his followers. Several of the people who took part in my research articulated the importance of Jesus as role model, especially in his need to take time away from his preaching, teaching and healing ministry in the presence of crowds and withdraw to spend time in prayer, alone or with a few disciples. This practice of resourcing himself regularly has inspired others to do the same, especially in monastic settings. God as Creator inhabits all our human creativity, so that by taking time to engage in creative repair we resource ourselves, especially when, like R. S. Thomas, we give ourselves to God's gaze. There are parallels between the artist sitting before a blank canvas and the practice of listening in the present moment to those whom we serve. Each involve a trust in the process, a unique now-ness of the encounter which thus allows God to work in us. There is indeed a theology of creative repair.

Creative Repair in Pastoral Practice

Creative repair as a concept and a practice has the capacity to help those who routinely find themselves helping others in a variety of contexts. Although I have focused my attention on clergy, especially those in the Church of England, due to the fact that my research produced evidence of their experience, my overall experience of psychotherapy and that of counsellor colleagues and teachers, and others in a caring role suggests that creative repair would help a wide range of people to resource themselves regularly.

As indicated in Chapter 2, the therapeutic value of the creative arts is evidenced by the established credibility of particular disciplines such as art therapy, music therapy and drama therapy. John Armstrong is a philosopher specializing in aesthetics and civilization. In a key book, he and a fellow philosopher, Alain de Botton, have argued that art *is* therapy (De Botton and Armstrong, 2013) and suggest that it is a tool with seven functions to help with seven identified 'psychological frailties' (p. 5). These are remembering, hope, sorrow, rebalancing, self-understanding, growth and appreciation. While these may be perceived as somewhat fragile, from the point of view of these two philosophers, sorrow as an expression of grief is more obviously recognized as a time of vulnerability and is often helpfully expressed in art. I have a beautiful original charcoal representation of Ruth and Naomi by the artist Davina Jackson, often commented on and identified with by my patients who are grieving. In it, a weeping Naomi is comforted by Ruth, and we can imagine Ruth's words, found in the book of Ruth, when she refuses to go back to her country of origin, as recommended by Naomi: 'Where you go, I will go; where you lodge, I will lodge, your people will be my people, your God my God' (Ruth 1.16).

Armstrong and de Botton suggest that 'art can ... teach us how to suffer more successfully' (2013, p. 26). They cite Richard Serra's *Fernando Pessoa* as telling us that 'Sorrow is written into the contract of life' (p. 26). It is addressed seriously in art often through a process of sublimation. Explaining that sublimation is a chemical term, a process by which a solid substance is transformed into gas without first becoming water, they suggest that it 'refers to the psychological process of transformation, in which base and unimpressive experiences are converted into something noble and fine — exactly what may happen when sorrow meets art' (p. 26).[1] While I would not describe experiences of loss and grief as in any way 'base', the idea that art can help a grieving person to feel less isolated and less despairing does make sense. An artist like Serra or Goldin seems to suggest that a sense of loss, disappointment and frustration is to be respected and may be accompanied and consoled by art. De Botton is also one of the founders of The School of Life, an educational company that offers advice on life issues. Their publication *Art Against Despair*, 'a portable museum dedicated to grief and courage' (2022, p. 4), is a book full of photographs of paintings and artefacts, each with a description offering comfort and consolation. The restorative use of images suggested by the work of Armstrong and de Botton also brings to mind the art of *kintsugi*, the Japanese process by which broken porcelain is repaired with gold, as discussed in Chapter 6.

The autumn 2022 edition of the quarterly *RA Magazine* published by London's Royal Academy of Arts included a debate on the question: 'Is looking at art a form of therapy?' John Armstrong, philosopher, and Lisa Appignanesi, writer on psychoanalysis, offer contrasting answers. Armstrong indicates that 'the idea that art is essentially therapeutic has been a consistent, underlying tenet of Western culture since antiquity' (Armstrong and Appignanesi, 2022, p. 35). He explains that the roots of art as therapy date to the discussion of poetry by Aristotle, who pioneered the idea that the arts can help the psyche, that is, mind or soul, at a time when 'therapy' was assumed to be a body-based treatment. Bemoaning the loss of this approach in more recent years, he concludes: 'To look at art as a form of therapy is – surprisingly – to reconnect with a central ambition of art: the guidance of our inner lives' (p. 35).

As a writer on psychoanalysis, Appignanesi accepts the role of art as an agent of transformation, yet she privileges the talking treatment, the importance of a live relationship with a trained professional, citing Freud's aim 'that the patient through the treatment would be better able to love and work' (p. 35). She adds: 'To be attentively heard, nudged into hearing oneself, redescribing difficulties, living old and new versions of our relations through the therapist, are part of therapy. And it all takes time' (p. 35). Yet she acknowledges that looking at art 'can elevate mood', impishly suggesting that 'GPs should be allowed to prescribe RA membership rather than anti-depressants' (p. 35).

I have cited this debate in some detail because it seems to indicate the therapeutic value of the arts, not as a substitute for rigorous psychotherapy but as a way of resourcing any of us, especially when we need a lift. Looked at through the lens of art as transformation, when encountered by sorrow art confronts reality, so links with one of Coutu's ingredients of resilience, as described in Chapter 8, as well as indicating the importance of the social dimension of humanity. In addition, art through its social expression eases the sense of isolation that often accompanies sorrow.

A life well lived

Following the death of Queen Elizabeth II, there were many tributes and comments on how she lived her life. It is possible to see aspects of creative repair in these various comments. For example, her love of animals, especially horses, was described and her passion for breeding racehorses and excitement when they were running seemed to resource her regularly. The annual retreat to Balmoral for special family time balanced her regular commitment to her royal duties. We have heard anecdotes of the way in which she put nervous people at their ease by asking them 'Where do you come from?' This may have also eased her own shyness, a creative response to these encounters, perhaps.[2]

It is worth pausing for a moment to reflect on the aftermath of the Queen's death during the official days of mourning. Collective grief was expressed in the queues to view her coffin in Edinburgh and London and in the crowds who travelled to witness the royal hearse as it made its way to and from airports in Edinburgh and Northolt and then to Buckingham Palace. Many people laid flowers, toys and messages and hundreds and thousands joined The Queue to 'pay their respects' as they filed through Westminster Hall in the days before the funeral in Westminster Abbey on 19 September 2022. What was going on? Some comparisons were made with the death and funeral of Princess Diana in 1997. As those professionally acquainted with the grieving process are aware, a recent loss can trigger an emotional connection with any previous losses. At one level, this is an echo of past sadness and unsurprising. However, if earlier losses have not been processed sufficiently, then a new loss can trigger a deeper or even catastrophic reaction because it is as if there is a shortcut to those deeper, insufficiently expressed feelings. For some this can even lead to a reactive depression and may call for professional help. Given that as a nation the British have valued stoicism characterized by the 'stiff upper lip', the death of the Queen has been an opportunity to join with others in a collective expression of grief.

The longevity of the Queen's reign and the consistency with which she lived out her early vow to serve her people for her whole life lead me to comment on the many tributes to her as the mother of the nation. Once again, I draw on the work of Winnicott, who was careful not to exclude fathers in his thinking and recognition of the contribution of his work and his 'urge to find and to appreciate the ordinary good mother'

(1986/1990, p. 123). He added: 'Fathers, I know, are just as important, and indeed an interest in mothering includes an interest in fathers, and in the vital part they play in child care' (p. 123). He was keen to 'draw attention to the immense contribution to the individual and to society that the ordinary good mother with her husband in support makes at the beginning, and which she does simply through being devoted to her infant' (p. 124).

The Queen and Prince Philip had their first experiences of parenting before the death of King George VI, which gave them a chance to establish themselves as parents. Although there would have been considerable practical help, it was a huge emotional challenge for Queen Elizabeth to combine the roles of sovereign and mother. When interviewed by Laura Kuenssberg on 18 September, Jacinta Ardern, Prime Minister of New Zealand, told of the importance of Queen Elizabeth as a role model for her as a national leader and mother. She was referring to the Queen having given birth to two later children, born some time after her coronation in 1953. Asked how she coped, the Queen replied that she 'just got on with it' (BBC, 2002, *Sunday with Laura Kuenssberg*). Over the 70 years of her reign, the Queen evolved her role, and the sheer longevity of her reign has meant that most people cannot remember a time without her maternal presence. Whether or not people value the monarchy as an institution, the massive expression of collective grief has suggested that her symbolic presence has been a constant in times of change and an example of soft power expressed through warmth, diplomacy, integrity and a genuine interest in each person she met. Her model of leadership has been praised by people throughout the world.

A flexible approach to leadership

As I indicated in Chapter 5, a flexible approach to leadership made possible by the decision of those in a leadership role to join creative repair groups as ordinary members helped them to sustain their roles. Several of those who took part in my research at various times drew on the example of Jesus as the ultimate role model. What Paul described as Christ's self-emptying, technically known as *kenosis*, in his call to the Philippians to practise humility (Phil. 2.5–8) has become an intentional example for many. This idea of servant-leadership is the espoused approach in many traditions. Living it out is not so easy, especially when recognizing that those in a leadership role, especially in a faith context, are on the receiving end of projections that can be difficult to manage. One of the checks and balances is the regular experience of being in a group with others as an ordinary member. If that is in the context of creative repair, then they are doubly nurtured by both the artform and the group.

In terms of the distribution of power, anyone who is offering help to others who are vulnerable needs not only to be a safe person to carry out the role, but also to be mindful of the power imbalance at work. This is why the quality of humility is so important in the Christian tradition. Charismatic leadership may be attractive to some, but it can be emotionally dangerous both to the leader and the led. One of the key values of the figure/ground approach in group analysis, as described in Chapter 5, is the built-in protection from self-idealization. Leadership can be burdensome and those called to it need to be encouraged to take due time off and enjoy interests and companionship that are outside the faith context. The same could be said for parents and those who care for others in any context. Respite care is essential for that care to be sustainable. Not only is this a chance to recharge batteries, but it is also a reminder that none of us is indispensable. Those in a leadership role have a duty to model good practice, and ideally this needs to be built into the process of clergy formation.

Implications for training and supervision

If creative repair is to become an integral part of well-being for pastoral carers, it needs to be built into the core training of all those who intend to offer such care. Although my primary experience is in the context of Anglican clergy, the principles may be applied to other settings. In any case one of my models of good practice is that of a rigorous psychotherapy or counselling training, in which the experience of having been in therapy and regular sessions in supervision are *de rigueur*. Leaders in most faith contexts expect to offer pastoral care to those they serve. While it can be assumed that their training will have included detailed study of their religious texts and many of the practical skills needed for their future role as faith leaders, it cannot be assumed that they will have had much in the way of training in pastoral skills. Also, pastoral supervision is a requirement in some denominations but optional in most. Supervision is a regular meeting with an approved supervisor who both understands the supervisee's ministry context and is able to think about pastoral situations with some distance from the setting involved.[3] It is not only a fruitful way of reflecting on the pastoral situation, but also acts as a check and balance against over-involvement. Also, it can help the pastoral carer to discern when a referral to a mental health professional is appropriate.

Long term, the importance of creative repair in its broadest sense needs to be modelled by those in senior positions. In the past, I have encountered an unhelpful tendency for clergy to boast of their busyness in a competitive way when they meet together. If only they would boast of the ways in which they have practised creative repair and encouraged others in their teams to do the same! This needs an intentional reflection on current practice and a critical analysis of the quality of training offered during both formation and later training. This brings me to my belief that, at a time when faith leaders can be spread over large distances with many congregations to support, it is time for what I would call a re-constellation of Christian practice. I leave it to others in their own faith contexts to reflect on their particular needs.

Time for a re-constellation of Christian practice

Although well-being and self-care are often referred to both in the public domain and in church conversations, for Christians the model of Jesus Christ is of paramount importance. While different denominations stress different aspects of his teaching and ministry, it is rare that his flexible approach to his ministry is highlighted. Of course, many monastic foundations have seen the importance of this, as I have stressed in Chapter 7. If we imagine the years in which Jesus had his own formation, we are told that he grew up in a devout family and probably learned the carpentry trade of his human father Joseph of Nazareth. As an elder brother, he would have observed the upbringing of his siblings and the importance of good mothering.

We get hints of Jesus' development of his religious faith from Luke's Gospel, when he stayed behind in Jerusalem engaging in theological debate with the religious teachers. This indicates the growing sense of his own future ministry, although we hear nothing more until his baptism by John, after which he goes into the wilderness to battle with his inner demons, the temptations of being spiritually gifted and charismatic and recognizing the need for a robust response. Only then did he call on others to join him, using language that would be understood by those whom he called to follow him. In other words, this was not an 'I'm in charge' approach. He chose to be part of a group and he chose to vary the times and places in which he taught and preached and healed the sick. Central to this was time apart with God, time in which to recover, rest and discern the way in which he was to handle those who found his ministry threatening to their sense of self-importance and pernickety interpretation of the Hebraic Law.

Throughout his ministry, Jesus confronted reality, including and especially when it was time to approach his own death.

He tried to prepare his disciples in advance and was at times frustrated by the gap between his own understanding of what was required and the human fallibility of those who did not want to lose him. He had no investment in being indispensable. Rather, he tried to train his disciples in the central need to proclaim the Kingdom of God. This included guidance not to waste time on those who did not welcome them and the helpful advice to be as 'wise as serpents and as innocent as doves' (Matt. 10.16).

If pastors are to sustain their precious ministry of being alongside others in their times of distress and grief, they must establish regular habits in order to avoid the accumulated stress that can lead to burnout. This is not an optional extra. Old habits such as 'going the extra mile' repeatedly, rather than as an exceptional response to an emergency, need to be replaced by an attitude that relies on the team or the group as a whole. Lone workers are particularly vulnerable to believing that they are irreplaceable.

Writing in *Reflections for Daily Prayer* on 'Who was I that I could hinder God?' (Acts 11.17), Rachel Mann warned against blocking the work of the Holy Spirit:

> While I suspect few of us deliberately wish to subvert God's love or get in his way, it is an ever-present temptation to identify what we want with what God desires. Ultimately, we are wise when we dare to let God lead. (2021, p. 257)

Most Christian pastors would acknowledge the role of the Holy Spirit, or, as John V. Taylor has described it, the 'Go-Between God' (1972). However, there are some who seem seduced by their own charisma. This can be especially tough for their spouses; I have known of situations in which self-regarding clergy have controlled their wives under the misapprehension that they are beyond accountability. In the selection process, such people can come across as very plausible, especially as many denominations seem to value charismatic preachers who have a powerful impact on their listeners. Selectors themselves need to be psychologically astute and model being at the same time both wise and harmless.

Conclusion

As Rowan Williams has put it: 'God has made us to live as material beings in a material world and has made us, therefore, as creatures who have to learn how to live in our world' (2007, p. 13). Creative repair in its broadest interpretation commits each of us to resourcing ourselves routinely as we seek to serve God and our neighbour in the various vocations to which God calls us. We need others, of course, whether they be partners, friends, colleagues and all those who are not afraid to speak truth to whatever power we are perceived to have. Not only do we need human friends but we can also be enriched by more abstract companions as can be found through reading or other creative pursuits. In his poem 'To a Young Beauty' (1968), W. B. Yeats wrote 'Choose your companions from the best', which might serve as a symbolic equivalent for those engaged in pastoral care. We find companions in the mind when we read a good book or listen to music or stand before a painting. By reading and being drawn into the poem by Yeats, I have lived out his advice in symbolic form and have repaired my inner resources. When I read a new book chosen by my book group, I am often challenged to try an author to whom I would not naturally gravitate and benefit from a group discussion that expands my horizons. When I go down to the allotment that I share with a friend, I meet other allottees who exchange good-humoured pleasantries and are always willing to help in a practical way. During the pandemic lockdowns these safe encounters were a lifeline. We have a duty to be good stewards of our physical health and mental well-being. Engaging in creative repair is one key way in which each of us can enjoy the world which God has created and contribute to our full flourishing.

Notes

1 De Botton and Armstrong illustrate this with reference to the painting by Nan Goldin, *Siobhan in My Mirror, Berlin 1992* (pp. 28–9).

2 I am grateful to my colleague Trisha Dale for this suggestion.

3 For more information on pastoral supervision, see Leach and Paterson, 2015.

Appendix A

Questions to Think About

These are ideas to mull over and think about – they do not require immediate answers.

1. How do you routinely restore your emotional and spiritual energy?
2. Is there any regular time given to participation in creative activity? For the purpose of this study, 'creative' is understood as pertaining to the creative arts, that is, literature, visual arts including photography, music and the performing arts.
3. How important is this time to you?
4. If you were to reflect theologically on this aspect of your life, what would your reference points be? Examples might be Gospel or other biblical texts, Christian tradition or literature or practice.
5. How does this activity enhance your ministry as a whole?
6. Some people, including clergy, who work in what might be described as 'the caring professions', suffer from 'compassion fatigue' or even 'burnout'. Do you have any thoughts about how this might be prevented? What part would more active participation in creative activity play in this?
7. Have you any additional responses to the ideas touched on in this discussion?

Appendix B

Informal Audit and Questions for Creative Repair

Creative repair is the regular engagement with the creative arts as a way of repairing or replenishing the resources poured out in sensitive pastoral care. 'Creative' is understood as pertaining to the creative arts, that is, literature, visual arts including photography, music and the performing arts. Resourcing includes all other ways of renewing physical, emotional and spiritual energy.

1. How do you routinely renew your physical, mental and emotional energy?
2. Do you have any assumptions about what resources you and what drains you? For example, if you like meeting friends on your day off, have you noticed how you feel afterwards?
3. What do you enjoy that could be described as creative repair?
4. How often are you able to engage in these activities?
5. Is this as often as you would like?
6. If not, what prevents you from practising creative repair?
7. If it is as often as you would like, what helps you?
8. Do you regard engaging in these things as:
    (a) Spiritual discipline?
    (b) Essential to the practice of ministry?
    (c) An unnecessary distraction?
    (d) A luxury that you cannot afford?

9. Do you have any other thoughts about your experience of creative repair?
10. Do you have any other thoughts about how you routinely resource yourself?

If you continue to review what resources you and what drains you and perhaps keep a creative repair journal or other record of your experiences, your understanding of your own resourcing needs will grow.

Bibliography

Allain-Chapman, J., 2012, *Resilient Pastors*, London: SPCK.

Allain-Chapman, J., 2018, *The Resilient Disciple*, London: SPCK.

Ansdell, G., 2015, *How Music Helps*, Farnham: Ashgate.

Armstrong, J., 2004/2005, *The Secret of Beauty*, London: Penguin Books.

Armstrong, J. and Appignanesi, L., 2022, Debate in *Royal Academy of Arts Magazine*, 156 (Autumn 2022).

Barnes, B., Ernst, S. and Hyde, K., 1999, *An Introduction to Groupwork: A Group-Analytic Perspective*, Basingstoke: Palgrave.

Begbie, J., 2001, 'Introduction' in J. Begbie (ed.), *Beholding the Glory*, Ada, MI: Baker Academic, pp. xi–xv.

Behr, H. and Hearst, L., 2005, *Group-Analytic Psychotherapy: A Meeting of Minds*, London: Whurr Publishers.

Bion, W. R., 1961, *Experiences in Groups*, New York: Basic Books.

Bion, W. R., 2014 (1967), 'A Theory of Thinking' in C. Mawson and F. Bion (eds), *The Complete Works of W.R. Bion*, London: Karnac.

Bloor, A., 2013, '"Who shall I be?" Putting on Priesthood in the Church of England' in T. Ling (ed.), *Moving On in Ministry*, London: Church House Publishing, pp. 17–30.

Bowlby, J., 1969, *Attachment and Loss: vol. 1 Attachment*, London: Hogarth.

Bowlby, J., 1979, *The Making and Breaking of Affectional Bonds*, London: Tavistock Publication.

Bragg, M., 1999 (Pbk. 2000), *The Soldier's Return*, London: Hodder and Stoughton/Sceptre.

Brother Roger, 2012, *Taizé*, London: SPCK.

Brown, D. and Peddar, J., 1991, *Introduction to Psychotherapy*, 2nd edn, London and New York: Tavistock/Routledge.

Butler Jr, L. H., 2012, 'Psychological Theory' in B. J. Miller-McLemore (ed.), *The Wiley-Blackwell Companion to Practical Theology*, Oxford: Wiley-Blackwell, pp. 102–11.

Cameron, H. and Duce, C., 2013, *Researching Practice in Ministry and Mission*, London: SCM Press.

Cherry, S., 2012, 'Time Wisdom' in T. Ling and L. Bentley (eds), *Developing Faithful Ministers*, London: SCM Press, pp. 97–107.

Church of England, 2014, *Criteria for Selection for the Ordained Ministry in the Church of England*, Ministry Division of the Archbishops' Council, https://www.churchofengland.org/sites/default/files/2017-10/selection_criteria_for_ordained_ministry.pdf (accessed 28.01.2018).

Cocksworth, C. and Brown, R., 2006, *Being a Priest Today*, 2nd edn, London: Canterbury Press Norwich.

Coles, R., 2022, *Murder Before Evensong*, London: Weidenfeld and Nicolson.

Collicutt, J., 2015, *The Psychology of Christian Character Formation*, London: SCM Press.

Coutu, D., 2017, 'How Resilience Works' in *Resilience*, Boston, MA: Harvard Business School, pp. 1–30.

Csikszentmihalyi, M., 1990, *Flow*, New York: Harper & Row.

Davies, H., 2022, 'To the Edge of Time and Space', *The Tablet*, 6 August, 276 (9464), pp. 4–5.

De Botton, A. and Armstrong, J., 2013, *Art is Therapy*, London: Phaidon.

De Caussade, J-P., 1981, *The Sacrament of the Present Moment*, translated by K. Muggeridge, London: Collins.

De Waal, E., 1995, *A Life-Giving Way*. London: Mowbray.

Dodge, R., Daly, A., Huyton, J. and Sanders, L., 2012, 'The Challenge of Defining Wellbeing', *International Journal of Wellbeing*, 2 (3), pp. 222–35.

Donne, J., 1623, 'Meditation XVII' in *Devotions Upon Emergent Occasions*, Amazon reprint.

Dunstan, P., 1997, *This Poor Sort*, London: Darton, Longman & Todd.

Eliot, T. S., 1959, *Four Quartets*, London: Faber.

Erikson, E., 1950, *Childhood and Society*, New York: Norton.

Esquerro, A., 2017, *Encounters with John Bowlby*, Abingdon: Routledge.

Farrington, K., 2020, *The Repair Shop. Tales from the Workshop of Dreams*, London: BBC Books.

Ford, D., 2012, *The Shape of Living*, London: SCM Press.

Foulkes, S. H., 1986, *Group Analytic Psychotherapy*, London: Karnac.

Frankl, V. E., 1959 edn, 2011, *Man's Search for Meaning*, London: Ryder.

Freud, S., 1984 [1923], *The Ego and the Id*, Penguin Freud Library, London: Penguin Books.

Freud, S., 1984 [1923], *Beyond the Pleasure Principle*, Penguin Freud Library, London: Penguin Books.

Freud, S., 1991 [1900], *The Interpretation of Dreams*, Penguin Freud Library, London: Penguin Books.

Gerhardt, S., 2004, *Why Love Matters*, Hove: Brunner-Routledge.

Gerity, L., 2000a, 'Preface' in E. Kramer (ed.), *Art as Therapy*, London: Jessica Kingsley, pp. 9–11.

Gerity, L., 2000b, 'Inner Satisfaction and External Success' in: E. Kramer (ed.), *Art as Therapy*, London: Jessica Kingsley, pp. 232–7.

Glenn, L., 1987, 'Attachment Theory and Group Analysis: The Group Matrix as a Secure Base', *Group Analysis*, 20 (2), pp. 109–26.

Gombrich, E. H., 1953, *The Story of Art*, London: Phaidon.

Graham, E., 1996, *Transforming Practice*, reprint 2002, Eugene, OR: Wipf & Stock.

Graham, E., Walton, H. and Ward, F., 2005, *Theological Reflection: Methods*, London: SCM Press.

Griffiths, A., *Refusing to be Indispensable*, Cambridge: Grove Books Limited.

Grosch-Miller, C. A., 2021, *Trauma and Pastoral Care*, London: Canterbury Press.

Handy, C., 1993, *Understanding Organisations*, 4th edn, London: Penguin Books.

Harries, R., 1993, *Art and the Beauty of God*, London: Cassell.

Holmes, A. C., 2011, 'Choose Your Companions from the Best', *Practical Theology*, 4 (1), pp. 67–81.

Holmes, J., 2001, *The Search for the Secure Base*, Hove: Routledge.

Hopper, E. and Weinberg, H. (eds), 2011, *The Social Unconscious in Persons, Groups and Societies, Volume 1: Mainly Theory*, London: Karnac.

Hurding, R., 2013, *Five Pathways to Wholeness*, London: SPCK.

Ison, D. (ed.), 2005, *The Vicar's Guide*, London: Church House Publishing.

Jacobs, M., 1986, *The Presenting Past*, London: Harper & Row.

Klein, M., 1975 (1946-63), *Envy, Gratitude and Other Works*. London: Hogarth Press and The Institute of Psychoanalysis.

Klein, M., 1992, *Love, Guilt and Reparation and Other Works 1921–1945*, London: Karnac.

Klein, M., Heimann, P. and Money-Kearle, R. (eds), 1955, *New Directions in Psycho-Analysis*, London: Tavistock Publications.

Kramer, E., 2000, *Art as Therapy*, London: Jessica Kingsley.

Lawson, F., 2005, 'Spiritual Life' in D. Ison (ed.), *The Vicar's Guide*, London: Church House Publishing, pp. 39–55.

Leach, J. and Paterson, M., 2015, *Pastoral Supervision*, 2nd edn, London: SCM Press.

Lyall, D., 2001, *Integrity of Pastoral Care*, London: SPCK.

MacCulloch, D., 2004, *Reformation*, London: Penguin Books.

MacGregor, N., 2010, *A History of the World in a Hundred Objects*, London: Allen Lane.

Malone, G., 2012, *Choir*, London: Collins

Mann, R., 2021, *Reflections for Daily Prayer*, London: Church House Publishing.

Marrone, M., 1994, 'Attachment Theory and Group Analysis' in D. Brown and L. Zinkin (eds), *The Psyche and the Social World*, London: Routledge, pp. 146–62.

Marrone, M., 2014, *Attachment and Interaction*, 2nd edn, London: Jessica Kingsley.

Maslow, A. H., 1954, *Motivation and Personality*, New York: Harper & Row.

McClure, B. J., 2010, *Moving Beyond Individualism in Pastoral Care and Counselling*, Eugene, OR: Cascade.

McGrath, A., 2022, *What's the Point of Theology?*, London: SPCK.

Mental Health Foundation, 2015, *Work Life Balance*.

Middleton, K., 2015, *Refuel*, London: Darton, Longman & Todd.

Miller-McLemore, B. J. (ed.), 2012, *The Wiley-Blackwell Companion to Practical Theology*, Oxford: Wiley-Blackwell.

Mitchell, J., 1998, 'Introduction to Melanie Klein' in J. Phillips and L. Stonebridge (eds), *Reading Melanie Klein*, London: Routledge, pp. 11–31.

Navarro, T., 2018, *Kintsugi*, London: Hodder and Stoughton.

Nouwen, H. J. M., 1979, *The Wounded Healer*, London: Darton, Longman and Todd.

O'Connor, E., 1975, *Journey Inward, Journey Outward*, New York: Harper & Row.

Paffenroth, K., 1999, *Allegorizations of the Active and Contemplative Lives in Philo, Origen, Augustine and Gregory*, available at https://www.bartleby.com/essay/Allegorizations-of-the-Active-and-Contemplative-Lives-FKCSPA2YTJ.

Pattison, S., 2007, *The Challenge of Practical Theology*, London: Jessica Kingsley.

Pedrick, C. and Clutterbuck, D., 2005, 'Professional and spiritual support' in J. Witcombe (ed.), *The Curate's Guide*, London: Church House Publishing, pp. 103–8.

Peyton, N. and Gatrell, C., 2013, *Managing Clergy Lives*, London: Bloomsbury.

Roberts, J., 1991, 'A View of the Current State of the Practice' in J. Roberts and M. Pines, *The Practice of Group Analysis*, London: Routledge, pp. 3–17.

Rose, J., 2013, *Psychology for Pastoral Contexts*, London: SCM Press.

Runcorn, D., 2005, 'Self-Management' in D. Ison (ed.), *The Vicar's Guide*, London: Church House Publishing.

Sayers, Dorothy L., 1994, *The Mind of the Maker*, London: Mowbray.

Segal, H., 1986, *The Work of Hannah Segal*, London: Free Association Books.

Segal, H., 1988, *Introduction to the Work of Melanie Klein*, London: Karnac and the Institute of Psychoanalysis.

Shipani, D. S., 2012, 'Case Study Method' in B. J. Miller-McLemore (ed.), *The Wiley-Blackwell Companion to Practical Theology*, Oxford: Wiley-Blackwell, pp. 91–101.

Skynner, R., 1989, *Institutes and How to Survive Them*, London: Methuen.

Society of St Francis, 2010, *The Daily Office*, London: Mowbray.

Stacey, R., 2003, *Strategic Management and Organisational Dynamics*, 4th edn, Harlow: Pearson Education.

Stanton, H., 2017, *For Peace and for Good*, London: Canterbury Press.

Storr, A., 1992, *Music and the Mind*, London: Harper Collins.

Swinton, J. and Mowat, H., 2006, *Practical Theology and Qualitative Research*, London: HarperCollins.

Symington, J. and Symington, N., 1996, *The Clinical Thinking of Wilfred Bion*, London: Routledge.

Taylor, John V., 1972, *The Go-Between God*, London: SCM Press.

Taylor, M., 2014, *Trauma Therapy and Clinical Practice: Neuroscience, Gestalt and the Body*, Maidenhead: Open University Press.

The School of Life, 2022, *Art Against Despair*, London: The School of Life.

Thomas, R. S., 1993, *Collected Poems 1945–1990*, London: Dent.

Tomlinson, Anne L., 2001, *Training God's Spies*, Edinburgh: Contact Pastoral Trust.

Tuckman, B., 1965, 'Developmental Sequence in Small Groups', *Psychological Bulletin*, 63 (6), pp. 384–99.

Turri, M., 2017, *Acting, Spectating and the Unconscious*, Abingdon: Routledge.

Walton, H., 2014, *Writing Methods in Theological Reflection*, London: SCM Press.

Watts, F., Nye, R. and Savage, S., 2002, *Psychology for Christian Ministry*, London: Routledge.

Webster, A., 2002, *Wellbeing*, London: SCM Press.

Williams, R., 2003, *Silence and Honeycakes*, Oxford: Lion.

Williams, R., 2007, 'A Theology of Health for Today' in J. Baxter (ed.), *Wounds that Heal*, London: SPCK, ch. 1.

Winkett, L., 2010, *Our Sound is Our Wound: Contemplative Listening to a Noisy World*, London: Continuum.

Winnicott, D., 1964, *The Child, the Family and the Outside World*, Harmondsworth: Penguin Books.

Winnicott, D., 1965/1990, *The Maturational Processes and the Facilitating Environment*, London: Karnac Books.

Winnicott, D., 1971/1991, *Playing & Reality*, London: Routledge.

Winnicott, D., 1986/1990, *Home is Where We Start From*, London: Penguin Books.

Woodward, J. and Pattison, S. (eds), 2000, *The Blackwell Reader in Pastoral and Practical Theology*, Oxford: Blackwell.

Yeats, W. B., 1968, *Selected Poetry*, London: Macmillan.

Index